twitter

tips, tricks, and

tweets

2nd Edition

twitter

tips, tricks, and

tweets

2nd Edition

Paul McFedries

WILEY

Wiley Publishing, Inc.

Twitter Tips, Tricks, and Tweets, 2nd Edition

Published by
Wiley Publishing, Inc.
10475 Crosspoint Blvd.
Indianapolis, IN 46256
www.wiley.com

For general information on our other products and services or to obtain technical support, please contact our Customer Care Department within the U.S. at (877) 762-2974, outside the U.S. at (317) 572-3993 or fax (317) 572-4002.

Wiley also publishes its books in a variety of electronic formats. Some content that appears in print may not be available in electronic books.

Library of Congress CIP Data: 2010926842

WILEY

About the Author

Paul McFedries is a technical writer who has been authoring computer books since 1991. He has more than 70 books to his credit, which together have sold more than three million copies worldwide. His current titles include the Wiley books *Internet Simplified*, *iPhone 3G S Portable Genius*, *Teach Yourself VISUALLY Macs*, and *Teach Yourself VISUALLY Windows 7*. Paul is also the proprietor of Word Spy, a Web site devoted to new words and phrases (see www.wordspy.com). Paul lives in Toronto with his wonderful wife, Karen, and their silly dog, Gypsy. Please visit Paul's personal website at www.mcfedries.com, or follow him on Twitter using his Twitter accounts @paulmcf and @wordspy.

Credits

Senior Acquisitions Editor
Jody Lefevere

Project Editor
Cricket Krengel

Development Editor
Kristin Vorce

Technical Editor
Jim Lefevere
jimlefevere.com

Copy Editor
Kim Heusel

Editorial Director
Robyn Siesky

Vice President and Group Executive Publisher
Richard Swadley

Vice President and Executive Publisher
Barry Pruett

Business Manager
Amy Knies

Senior Marketing Manager
Sandy Smith

Project Coordinator
Patrick Redmond

Graphics and Production Specialists
Andrea Hornberger

Quality Control Technician
Melanie Hoffman

Proofreading
Melissa D. Buddendeck

Indexing
Potomac Indexing, LLC

To Karen, who follows my offline tweets.

Acknowledgments

Many writers believe that the essence of good writing is rewriting. Not me. I believe that the essence of good writing is good *editing*. I don't care how talented you are as a writer and how many times you rewrite each sentence, a good editor will make your writing better, period. Of course, there's a lot riding on that little word "good." Fortunately, the editorial team at Wiley is one of the best in the business. The book's Project Editor was Cricket Krengel, who easily qualifies as a *great* editor, and I send along a thousand, nay a *million* thank-yous to her for bringing this book up to a level beyond its author. I had the distinct pleasure of working with Kristin Vorce, the book's Development Editor, who was bubbling over with great ideas and suggestions. As you read this book, you'll notice that every i is dotted and every t is crossed, and for that I extend heartfelt thanks to this book's Copy Editor, the sharp-eyed Kim Heusel. Technical writing must be technically accurate, of course, or there's just no point to it. So for the often thankless tasking of taking all my techniques for a test drive, I thank this book's Technical Editor, Jim Lefevere. Finally, I would be remiss if I didn't also shout "Thank you!" at the top of my lungs to this book's Acquisitions Editor, Jody Lefevere, for asking me to write the book. I can't tell you how much fun I had writing it.

foreword

Social media is a phenomenon that's turning everyone into a publisher and distributor of media: from YouTube videos to blog posts to Twitter messages and even comments on the articles we read around the web, we're all becoming content creators. As the CEO and founder of Mashable. com, an online guide to social media, I've seen this trend evolve from the clunky old blogging software of years ago — for which you needed to understand web hosting and basic programming to even get started — to the effortless simplicity of a 140-character Twitter message (or Tweet).

Twitter is perhaps the simplest and most addictive social media tool of them all, and its unprecedented success has been both unexpected and inspirational. I've been fortunate to be part of that journey, tracking Twitter's growth on behalf of Mashable and posting updates about Twitter and social media to the @mashable Twitter account.

As you'll learn in this book, once the basic principles of Twitter are understood, the possibilities are almost limitless. In fact, much of the service's appeal comes from its simplicity: write anything you wish in 140-characters or less, and then share it with the world. Is it a chat room? Is it a way to send text messages to a group of friends? Is it a new technology for reading news headlines? Is it the world's simplest social network, a barebones version of MySpace and Facebook? It's all of those things and more: Twitter is whatever you make it.

Twitter is only four years old, but the service has been put to some inspirational, innovative and quirky uses already. Surgeons have Tweeted live from the operating room. A worldwide fundraising event was organized, garnering more than $250,000 for charity. More than one marriage proposal has been made (and accepted!). A British man traveled around the world to New Zealand, getting by thanks to the kindness of Twitter users. And in thousands of cities, Twitter fans have come together in real life Tweetups, making their virtual connections real.

Twitter's users are exceptionally inventive and resourceful, too. An expectant father created a device for his pregnant wife to wear: it sends a Twitter message every time their baby kicks. A software developer created a system that turns the lights on or off in his home by sending out a Tweet. You can even buy a kit for your plants that posts a Tweet when they need watering; a similar kit allows you to track your power consumption via Twitter.

Tweeting plants aren't the only non-human Twitter members. Both the Space Shuttle Endeavour and Mars Phoenix Lander posted Tweets during their missions for NASA, while London's Tower Bridge posts a Tweet when it opens or closes. There are Tweets from a whale on the ceiling of the Natural History Museum in New York City. And one of Twitter's most popular users is a cat in Waltham, Massachusetts.

All this innovation and creativity is part of Twitter's culture, it seems: a wealth of Tweet-powered services have sprung up, creating a flourishing ecosystem of so-called Twitter applications. There are tools to find Twitter users near you; Web sites that list the funniest Tweets (or the most insightful); services that rank Twitter users by their influence; and three-dimensional maps that show Tweets being posted around the world, every minute of the day.

More remarkable than all of these developments, however, is Twitter's profound effect on society: from news coverage to politics to customer relations and the nature of celebrity, this seemingly simple service is transforming entire industries.

Newspapers use Twitter as both a source of stories and a way to distribute their own headlines. Many of the top Twitter users are news agencies, and Twitter members have been known to Tweet about breaking news hours before its coverage on television. The effect on the media has been so dramatic; in fact, that one UK newspaper posted an April's Fool's joke claiming that it would cease publication of the paper and publish stories solely in Tweeted form.

News and politics go hand in hand, and politicians are equally cognizant of Twitter's power: US President Barack Obama has an enormous Twitter following, and his team posts occasional updates that request feedback from the American public. Obama is the most prominent among hundreds of Twittering politicians from numerous countries and political persuasions; of course, Twitter is non-partisan and international in its scope.

If Twitter can influence our political opinions, could it also determine what we buy? Some of the world's biggest brands hope so, and many have jumped into Twitterland with both feet. Some use the service for product announcements, while others post responses to questions and complaints from customers; some even host contests to win free products and services.

What about personal branding and celebrity? From Hollywood stars to sporting heroes to the world's most famous musicians, Twitter provides a connection between celebrities and their fans that is more direct than ever before. Some of the world's most recognizable names are using Twitter, giving us unprecedented insights into their everyday lives.

That's just a sampling of what you'll find on Twitter; it's inspiration, information, news, gossip, humor and remarkable personal stories. Twitter is all that we are, from our most exalted moments to our most mundane — and everything in between.

~ Pete Cashmore, CEO and founder of Mashable.com

contents

introduction

When I wrote the first edition of this book, Twitter was just starting to hit the big time: bemused front page articles in just about every magazine and newspaper in the land wondered just what this Twitter thing was all about; the actor Ashton Kutcher (@aplusk) had just cracked the one million follower mark; and Oprah herself had joined the fray with her own Twitter account (@oprah).

A year later, has anything changed? Oh, just a few things: Now every magazine and newspaper in the land not only has its own Twitter feed, but most of their reporters and writers have Twitter accounts, too; more than *two hundred* Twitter users have at least one million followers; and, of course, anybody who is anyone now tweets.

In fact, as I was writing this edition Twitter crossed the 100 million user threshold, a jaw-dropping number that, more than anything else, signals Twitter's newfound (and apparently permanent) place in the mainstream. That's a pretty heady climb for a service that began with the question "What are you doing?," a query so humble and mundane that Twitter was either ridiculed or ignored for most of its early life.

What turned the tide? The overall rise of social networking sure helped, of course, but I think the real secret of Twitter's success is that the Twitter users took the original *What are you doing?* question and morphed it into something more along the lines of *What's happening now?* (In fact, as you see in Chapter 3, Twitter recently changed the question from *What are you doing?* to *What's happening?*) That seemingly subtle change has made all the difference because it opens up a world of new questions: What are you reading? What great idea did you just come up with? What are you worried about? What interesting person did you just see or hear? What great information did you stumble upon on the Web? What hilarious video would you like to share?

Yes, you can still tell people what you're doing, and lots of Twitter users do just that. What's different now is that you're free to turn your Twitter experience into anything you want it to be. To do that, however, you need a guide to the ins and outs of Twitter and the tools, services, and sites that have sprung up in its wake. That's what *Twitter Tips, Tricks, and Tweets, Second Edition* aims to be. This book not only tells you everything you need to know to get started with Twitter and perform all of its standard chores, but it goes beyond the basics to show you how to wring every last bit of usefulness, education, and fun out of Twitter.

Who should read this book? You!

Some books are aimed squarely at specific types of people: beginners, programmers, left-handers, or whatever. Not this book:

- If you've never even heard of Twitter until this second, you can safely use this book to get started and see what all the fuss is about.
- If you've used Twitter for a while but haven't explored much, this book will be the map that shows you how to get to Twitter's useful and fun features and tools.
- If you already know your way around Twitter, I'm confident that this book will tell you a few things you don't know and will introduce you to some techniques you haven't yet tried.
- If you hate Twitter or are simply mystified by the whole thing, I hope this book will show you that although Twitter isn't the life-changing event that some folks make it out to be, it is useful and entertaining if you use it in a way that suits you.

That's all for now. I hope you enjoy the book.

Happy Twittering!

How Do I Get Started with Twitter?

1234567889

Are you ready to share with the world select bits and pieces of your life, 140 characters (or less) at a time? I suspected as much. This means that you're ready to get started with Twitter, the microblogging service that has taken the online world by storm. In this chapter, you begin, appropriately enough, at the beginning by learning how to set up and sign in to a Twitter account. Even if you've already got a Twitter account up and running, this chapter also takes you through a few other crucial Twitter techniques, including changing and resetting your Twitter password.

Setting Up Your Very Own Twitter Account

If all you want out of Twitter is to read a particular Twitterer's updates, then you don't need to bother creating your own account. Instead, point your favorite Web browser to http://twitter.com/*user*, where *user* is the person's user name on Twitter, and then peruse the updates that appear on the page.

This, of course, is no fun whatsoever. Twitter is all about sharing and participating in a community of fellow Twitterheads, and you can't do either of those things if you're sitting on the sidelines. Even better, joining Twitter literally takes only seconds of your time. So, without further ado (not that there's been much ado so far), here's how to join Twitter:

1. **Display Twitter's Create an Account page by navigating your Web browser to http://twitter.com/signup.** If you're already on http://twitter.com, click Join today; if you're already viewing a Twitterer's updates, click the Join today button.

2. **Use the Full name text box to type the name that you want other people to see when they look at your Twitter profile.** Two things to consider here

   - If you want people to find you on Twitter, be sure to type both your first and last names.

   - You can't include the text *twitter* anywhere in the name.

   - The maximum number of characters you can type is 20.

3. **In the Username text box, type the username you want to use on Twitter.** Here are some notes to bear in mind:

   - The username defines your Twitter address (it's http://twitter.com/*username*), it appears before each of your updates, and it appears in various other places in the Twitter landscape, so pick something you like and that has meaning.

   - The maximum number of characters is 15.

   - You can include any combination of letters, numbers, and underscores (_). All other characters are illegal (you can't even type them in the text box).

   - You can't include the text *twitter* anywhere in the username.

   - As you type, Twitter checks to see if your username is available. If you see username has already been taken, then you're out of luck and need to try again. If you see "ok" then you're good to go.

Don't sweat the username choice too much because you can always change it later.

4. **Use the Password text box to type a password for your Twitter account.** More informational notes

  ○ The password must be at least six characters long.

  ○ As you type the password, Twitter rates the password strength: Too obvious (if it's the same as your username, which is *not* a good idea!), Weak, Good, Strong, or Very Strong. To get your password up to the Very Strong rating, make the password at least eight characters long, and include at least one number and one nonalphanumeric symbol.

5. **In the Email text box, type the e-mail address you want to use to receive Twitter notifications and other messages.** You learn in Chapter 2 how to customize these notifications. If you want to receive the Twitter newsletter, be sure to select the I want the inside scoop check box. Figure 1.1 shows a Create an Account page ready for action.

twitter

Join the Conversation

Already on Twitter? Sign in.

☀ Already use Twitter on your phone? Finish signup now.

Full name	**Aardvaark Sorenstam**	✔ ok
Username	**aardvaarksorens**	✔ ok
	Your URL: http://twitter.com/ **aardvaarksorens**	
Password	●●●●●●●●●●	✔ Very Strong
Email	**asorenstam@tuborg.com**	✔ ok

☑ Let others find me by my email address
Note: Email will not be publicly displayed

Terms of Service Printable version

Terms of Service

These Terms of Service ("Terms") govern your access to and use of the services and Twitter's websites (the "Services"), and

By clicking on "Create my account" below, you are agreeing to the Terms of Service above and the Privacy Policy.

Create my account

☑ I want the inside scoop—please send me email updates!

1.1 Twitter's Create an Account page with all fields neatly filled in

6. **Click Create my account.** Twitter does just that, and it then offers to look for your friends on services such as AOL and Hotmail.

7. **You learn how to do this in Chapter 4, so click Skip this step.** Twitter displays a list of famous, semifamous, or just plain infamous people who are on Twitter and asks if you want to follow them.

8. **Again, you learn how to follow the famous in Chapter 4, so click Skip this step.** Do *not* click Finish here, or else you'll end up following all 20 people! Twitter finalizes your account and drops you off on your Twitter home page.

Signing In to Your Twitter Account

With your shiny, new Twitter account fully formed and primed for action, you're ready to venture into the Twitterverse. Twitter is kind enough to deliver you to your home page right after it creates your account, so if that's where you are now you can skip ahead.

However, after you end your browser session and start a new one, you'll need to sign in to your Twitter account once again. Follow these steps to not only sign in, but also to tell Twitter to remember your credentials so you don't have to bother with this again (at least when using the same browser on the same computer):

1. **Send your trusty Web browser to https://twitter.com/login.** You can also click the Login link that appears on just about every Twitter page.

2. **Type your Twitter username in the Username text box.**

3. **Type your Twitter password in the Password text box.**

4. **Select the Remember me check box.** This tells Twitter to add a cookie to your computer that saves your username and password, which enables you to log in automatically in the future.

5. **Click Sign in.**

6. **If you started off in some other Twitter page, Twitter redisplays that page, so click Home to get to your account's home page.**

Viewing Twitter's Current Status

Twitter puts the fun in funky and the hip in friendship, but it can also sometimes put the ugh in ugly. I'm talking here about Twitter's occasional reliability problems. Twitter's original infrastructure wasn't built to handle the massive amount of traffic it now bears, so every so often there will be a hiccup, a glitch, or even an outright failure.

These failures arise when Twitter's server simply gets overloaded, so it can't process any new data until some processing power is freed up. You know this is the case when you try to do something on Twitter and you see, instead, the infamous *fail whale*, as shown in Figure 1.2.

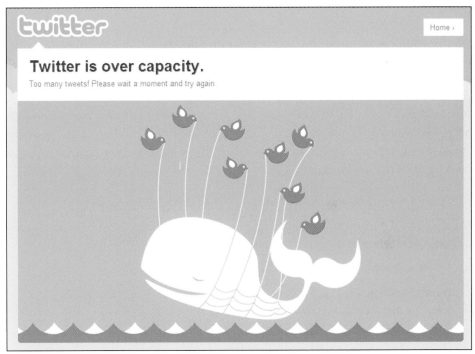

1.2 If Twitter gets overwhelmed by updates, the impossible-not-to-love fail whale shows up to let you know.

The good news is that the fail whale's moment on the stage is almost always mercifully brief, so you should be able to continue what you were doing in a few seconds or, at most, a few minutes.

You'll also be happy to know that our friend the fail whale shows up far less often than he (she?) used to. Over the past year or so, Twitter has made impressive strides in not only plugging the leaks but also shoring up the foundations, so the service is now more reliable than ever.

Unfortunately, that doesn't mean it's 100% reliable (online, nothing is). The fail whale still drops by unannounced on occasion, but Twitter also suffers from other gremlins from time to time. For example, you might see the whimsically mysterious Something is technically wrong page, as shown in Figure 1.3, if Twitter blows the online equivalent of a gasket.

So it pays to keep on top of Twitter's current status. There are a couple of ways you can do this.

1.3 If a wrench gets thrown into the Twitter works, you might see this page.

First, send your Web browser to http://status.twitter.com/ to open the Twitter Status page, which displays updates on Twitter's woes and worries, as shown in Figure 1.4.

Alternatively, visit the @twitter account by checking out http://twitter.com/twitter, shown in Figure 1.5.

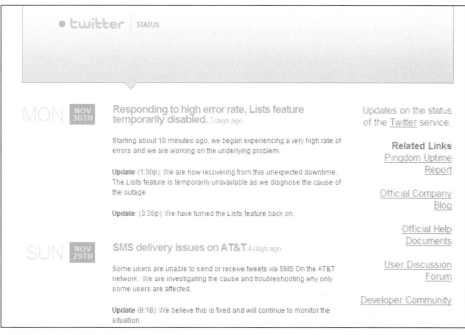

1.4 Drop by the Twitter Status page to keep an eye on Twitter's health.

Ideally, you should follow @twitter so you see the service updates automatically. See Chapter 4 to learn how to follow folks on Twitter.

If you're wondering about the @ symbol that appears periodically throughout the book, know it's a kind of Twitter shorthand that means "the Twitterer with the username." So @twitter means "the Twitterer with the username twitter."

1.5 Check out the @twitter account for the latest updates on the Twitter service.

Changing Your Twitter Password

When you forged your new Twitter account, you had to specify an account password, and Twitter is security-minded enough to rate your password on the fly: Too obvious, Weak, Good, Strong, or Very Strong. If you settled for a Weak or even just a Good rating, you might be having second thoughts and feel you'd sleep better at night with a Strong or even a Very Strong password.

Conversely, you might be wondering what's the big whoop about a Twitter password? After all, it's just your Twitter account. It's not like you're exposing your finances or national security secrets to the world (I'm assuming here you're not the Secretary of State). True enough, but it's also true that Twitter accounts have been hacked in the past, with the accounts of Britney Spears and a Twitter staffer (who was using the password "happiness," which is about as weak as they come) being the most notorious. If you're using your real name with your Twitter account, then you definitely don't want some malicious hacker having his way with this part of your online identity.

Fortunately, changing the password for your Twitter account isn't much harder than what you had to go through in the first place:

1. **Sign in to your Twitter account.**

2. **Click Settings.** The Settings page appears.

3. **Click the Password tab.**

4. **Use the Current Password text box to type your existing Twitter password.**

5. **Type your new password in the New Password and Verify New Password text boxes.**

6. **Click Change.** Twitter updates your account with the new password.

Resetting Your Twitter Password

Okay, so you've been on vacation for a couple of weeks, or your nose has been grindstone-bound while you finish off a few projects, and you've been away from the Twitterverse for a bit. It happens even to the most dedicated Twitterers. You return to the login screen and, doh!, you've forgotten your password. You try all your old favorites, but no joy. You're locked out of your Twitter account!

Fortunately, all is not lost. You can ask the kind folks at Twitter to reset your password, which will get you back up and tweeting in just a few minutes. Here's what you do:

1. **Send your Web browser to https://twitter.com/account/resend_password.** The Forgot your password? page appears.

2. **Type your Twitter username in the text box.** You can also type the e-mail address that you associated with your Twitter account.

3. **Click Send instructions.** Twitter ships you an e-mail message (Subject line: "Reset your Twitter password") that includes a link to a password reset page.

4. **When you get the message, click the link.** Your default Web browser pops up and takes you to the password reset page.

5. **Type your new password in the New Password and Verify New Password text boxes.**

6. **Click Change.** Twitter resets your account with the new password.

Deleting Your Twitter Account

I have the feeling that you're going to love Twitter, but it's also true that microblogging isn't for everyone. The constant pressure to answer the canonical Twitter question "What's happening?" may simply become too much after a while. If taking a short break doesn't help (I'm talking about a few days or even a few weeks, not a few minutes), then you can walk away and move on with your life. You could opt to let your account lie dormant (it is, after all, free), but if there are updates you want to get rid of, or if you don't want new people to follow you, then you should delete your Twitter account.

Of course, it could be that you love the whole Twitter thing, perhaps even to the extent that you've created multiple Twitter accounts. Lots of people juggle multiple Twitter identities (I have two, myself), but it requires lots of logging in and out, and lots of extra work updating and maintaining each account. If it all just gets to be too much, you might want to delete one or more of your accounts so you can finally get some sleep at night.

If you need to go the multiple-account route, then I strongly suggest using a third-party tool that supports multiple Twitter accounts, such as TweetDeck. See Chapter 8 for a look at some of these powerful tweeting tools.

Fortunately, unlike a lot of online services that bury their account-removal features in some obscure nook or cranny of their site (or, worse, require you to call the company to have your account terminated), Twitter makes it nearly painless to delete an account. Here's what you do:

1. **Sign in to your Twitter account.**
2. **Click Settings.** The Settings page appears.
3. **Click the Account tab.**
4. **Near the bottom of the page, click the Deactivate my account link.** The Is this goodbye? page appears, which asks if you really want to go through with this.
5. **Click Okay, fine, deactivate my account.** Twitter deletes your account.

Did you click the Okay, fine, deactivate my account button and then immediately regret your rash decision? Not to worry, because Twitter actually keeps your account in limbo for six months. If you change your mind within that time, you can get your deleted account restored with almost no fuss.

1. **Direct your nearest Web browser to http://twitter.com/account/deleted.**

2. **Use the text box to type the username or e-mail address associated with the account.**

3. **Click Restore my account.** You'll receive an e-mail message that offers a link, and you click that link to restore your account.

Yes, it is really that easy, providing you restore it when your account is still in that limbo period.

What Can I Do to Customize My Twitter Profile?

1 2 3 4 5 6 7 8 9

When you first sign up with Twitter, your account is about as bare-bones as it gets. You have no updates, no replies, no direct messages, no followers, and no one who you're following. Zeroes across the board! You soon fix all that. For now, though, you need to get ready to meet your public. This means taking a few minutes to customize your Twitter profile by filling in some of the missing details, choosing your all-important picture, sprucing up your Twitter home with colors and a background image, and configuring how Twitter notifies you of account events.

Filling In Your Profile Details

When you created your Twitter account, you only had to specify four things about yourself: your name, the Twitter username you preferred, a password for your account, and your e-mail address. That made the signup procedure blessedly quick, but it doesn't give folks much to chew on when they access your profile. Fortunately, Twitter lets you fill in a few more details after your account is set up, including your time zone, your Web site address, a short bio, your location in the real world, and the language you prefer. Of these, your Web address, bio, and location are the most important because they appear directly on your Twitter home page (as does your real name), so anyone (even nontweeters) can see them.

Here are the steps to follow to fill in these profile details:

1. **Sign in to your Twitter account.**

2. **Click Settings.** The Settings page appears.

3. **Click the Profile tab.**

4. **If you want to adjust your real name, edit the Name text box.** Remember that other Twitter users usually rely on the real name to find people, so don't be shy about using your full name (although remember that you only get 20 characters to play with here).

5. **Use the Location text box to type your city, state, country, GPS coordinates, or any combination of the four (up to 30 characters).**

6. **If you have a separate Web site or blog, use the Web text box to type the address.** Twitter displays this address as a link on your Twitter home page so folks can easily click over to your site.

7. **In the one line Bio text box, type a short description of yourself.** Somewhat oddly, Twitter gives you 160 characters here; limiting this field to 140 characters would seem more in keeping with the Twitter vibe, but there you go. Figure 2.1 shows a Profile tab with the various fields filled in.

8. **Click the Account tab.**

9. **If you want to change the e-mail address that Twitter uses to communicate with you, edit the Email text box.** Although you may be tempted to use a fake address here, stick with a legit address to ensure not only that you get notifications from Twitter, but also so you have the option of resetting your password if you forget it (as described in Chapter 1).

10. **Use the Time Zone list to choose the option that most closely matches your time zone.**

11. **Click Save.** Twitter updates your profile.

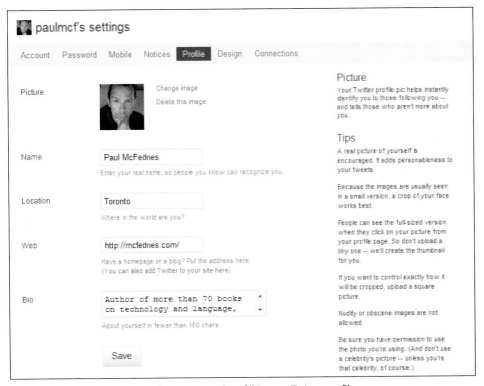

2.1 Click Settings, and then use the Account tab to fill in your Twitter profile.

Give a bit of time and thought to your Twitter bio. When people are deciding whether to follow you, they look at your recent tweets, for sure, but most folks also glance at the bio to get a sense of who you are. If your bio is uninspiring, people might think your tweets will be, too. A bio that portrays a sense of whimsy or fun is always welcome in the Twittersphere.

To take a peek at your newly renovated profile, click the Profile link. Figure 2.2 shows a Twitter profile page with the account's real name, location, Web site address (as a link), and bio.

Setting Your Twitter Picture

If the eyes are the windows of the soul, your Twitter picture is the window of your account. Sort of. To see what I mean, check out the list of tweeters shown in Figure 2.3 (this is a list of the people a particular account is following). See the picture in the lower-right corner? That's the generic image that Twitter displays when a user hasn't taken the time to choose his or her own picture.

Of course, no one's going to put a gun to your head to force you to put up your own picture, but that generic image is rather lame, and it tells folks that you haven't got your act together enough to spend the couple of minutes that it takes to set your own picture. (Even worse, most Twitter spammers don't bother setting their account picture, so many tweeters automatically think "Spammer!" when they see the generic picture icon.) Even better, choosing your own picture is a chance to have a bit of fun. Most tweeters use simple head shots of themselves, but a large percentage use something else entirely: a cartoon character, a caricature, an animal, a logo, or whatever. Feel free to let your imagination run a bit wild here.

After you settle on an image that suits your style, follow these steps to add it to your profile:

1. **Sign in to your Twitter account.**

2. **Click Settings.** The Settings page appears.

3. **Click the Profile tab.**

Name Paul McFedries
Location Toronto
Web http://mcfedries....
Bio Author of more than 70 books on technology and language, including Twitter Tips, Tricks, and Tweets!

32	592	8
following	followers	listed

2.2 Your profile page proudly displays your name, location, Web site address, and bio.

2.3 The image in the lower-right corner is what Twitter displays when an account has no picture set up.

4. **Click Change image.**

5. **Click Browse.** If you're using Safari, click Choose File instead. A file selection dialog box appears.

6. **Choose the file you want to use, and then click Open (or Choose in Safari).** You can use a JPEG, PNG, or GIF file, and the maximum size is 700K.

7. **Click Save.** Twitter updates your profile with the new image, although sometimes this takes a few minutes, depending on what mood the Twitter servers are in that day.

Although you might think you need to use a tiny image for Twitter, you can load a larger image if you want. Twitter shrinks it down to size in your profile, but folks can click the image to see it full size.

Applying a Theme to Your Profile

Your fresh-out-of-the-box Twitter account sets up your pages to use a collection of colors and images that are the same for all new accounts:

- The page background is mostly light blue.
- The page background shows faint cloudlike images.
- The sidebar uses a light-blue background.
- The sidebar border is also light blue.
- The links are a darker blue.
- The text is dark gray.

Taken together, these half-dozen items comprise the profile's *theme*. Happily, you're not stuck with the default theme. If you want to give your Twitter profile a different look, you can apply one of the 20 prefab themes that Twitter provides, or you can take an even more customized approach by choosing your own theme components.

The next couple of sections take you on this theme road less traveled, but for now here are the steps to follow to apply a predefined Twitter theme:

1. **Sign in to your Twitter account.**

2. **Click Settings.** The Settings page appears.

3. **Click the Design tab.**

4. **In the Select a theme area, click a theme that looks promising.** Twitter applies the theme temporarily, as shown in Figure 2.4.

5. **Repeat step 4 until you find a theme that suits your style.**

6. **Click Save Changes.** Twitter updates your profile with the new theme.

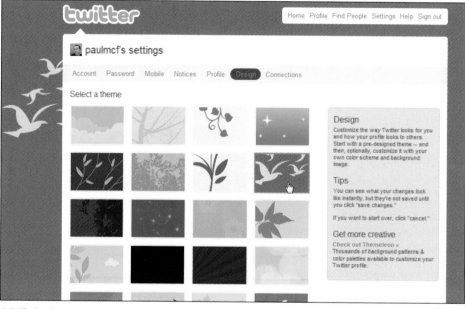

2.4 Click a theme thumbnail and Twitter applies the background and colors temporarily.

Selecting a Background Image

Applying a predefined Twitter theme is an easy way to escape the standard-issue look of a freshly minted Twitter account, but it doesn't exactly scream "rugged individualist." If you really want to stand out from the Twitter herd, then you need to customize your theme with your own background and (as I describe later) your own color scheme.

You may be wondering at this point why you should bother taking the time and trouble to build a custom theme. First, as you'll soon see, it doesn't take all that much time and it's almost no trouble. Second, even if it doesn't bother you to stick with a cookie-cutter theme from Twitter, it's not going to impress other tweeters, and that may be the deciding factor when they're choosing whether to follow your tweets (which are the updates you post). After all (a Twitterer might say), if you can't be bothered to do something original and interesting with your theme, then perhaps your tweets won't be all that original and interesting, either. Myself, I think that most tweeters decide on who to follow based on the quality of a person's updates, not on the appeal (or lack thereof) of their theme, but certainly there's no harm in making your Twitter home look nice.

Using a solid-color background

The simplest customization you can make to your design is to switch to a solid-color background. Swirling patterns and striking photos have their place in the world of Twitter backgrounds, but some people find them distracting. Framing your Twitter home with an attractive color lays a solid foundation for your content and focuses your reader's attention on your posts.

The section of the page where your tweets appear always has a white background, so you can give your profile an attractively clean and classily simple look by switching to a white background.

Here are the steps you have to follow to switch to a solid-color background:

1. **Sign in to your Twitter account.**

2. **Click Settings.** The Settings page appears.

3. **Click the Design tab.**

4. **If you have a predefined Twitter theme applied, click Change background image, and then click Don't use a background image.**

5. **Click Change design colors.**

6. **Click the background swatch.** Twitter displays two color controls, as shown in Figure 2.5. The narrow strip in the middle controls the base color, and the large square controls the amount of gray in the color.

7. **Click a spot in the strip to set the base color.** You can also drag either of the two arrows to set the base. When you make your choice, Twitter temporarily changes the background color so you can see the results.

If you happen to know the color code of the shade you want, you can type it directly in the background swatch. Be sure to use the format rrggbb, where rr is a two-digit hexadecimal value (00 to 99 and AA to EE) that specifies the red component, gg is a two-digit hexadecimal value that specifies the green component, and bb is a two-digit hexadecimal value that specifies the blue component.

8. **Click a spot in the large square to set the gray component color.** You can also drag the small circle to set the grayness. Again, Twitter temporarily changes the background color so you can see the results.

9. **Click Done.**

10. **Click Save Changes.** Twitter updates your profile with the new background color.

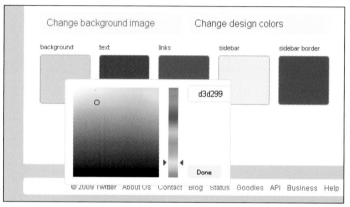

2.5 Click Change design colors and then use the color pickers to choose the color you want.

Selecting a custom background image

If you want to ramp up the "wow" factor, if you want to use your Twitter profile as part of a personal or business branding strategy, or if you just want a Twitter home that truly reflects your style and personality, then you need to augment your design with a custom background image.

You might think this is just a simple matter of uploading your favorite photo, but Twitter offers several unique challenges when it comes to selecting a background image. Before I get to those, here are the steps you need to follow to apply a custom background image to your Twitter profile:

1. **Sign in to your Twitter account.**

2. **Click Settings.** The Settings page appears.

3. **Click the Design tab.**

4. **Click Change background image.** Twitter prompts you to specify a file.

5. **Click Browse.** If you're using Safari, click Choose File instead. A file selection dialog box appears.

6. **Choose the file you want to use, and then click Open (or Choose in Safari).** You can use a JPEG, PNG, or GIF file, and the maximum size is 800K.

7. **If you want Twitter to tile the image to cover the background, select the Tile Background check box.**

8. **Click Save Changes.** Twitter updates your profile with the new background image.

After you save your profile, you might end up on the Something is technically wrong page or even the fail whale page. This is an annoyingly common problem, and the best solution is to keep refreshing your browser until Twitter gets its act together. Note that when you refresh, your browser asks whether you want to resubmit the form, so be sure to choose Yes.

Background photo challenges

As I mentioned earlier, Twitter presents a couple of hurdles that you need to leap over when selecting a background image. First, the Twitter content area — the box in the middle of the screen that displays your tweets and the Twitter sidebar — is a "fixed" target that you have to work around. I put "fixed" in quotation marks because it does move from side to side as you change your browser width or screen resolution, and it does expand vertically as you add tweets to your profile and as you start receiving other people's tweets on your home page. However, the content area is fixed in three other ways:

- It's always centered on the screen.
- It's always the same width: about 760 pixels.
- It's always located in the same position vertically: about 60 pixels from the top of the page.

This means that your background image has to deal with a distressingly large object. For example, on a screen with a resolution of 1024 × 768 with the browser window maximized, as shown in Figure 2.6, you have about 120 pixels of open area to the left of the content box and about 120 open pixels to the right of the content. You also have about 60 pixels open above the content box, but that area is partially blocked by the Twitter logo and the site navigation tools.

So if you want to use a photo as your background, then even if you use an image large enough to cover the screen, the bulk of the image will be blocked, which is going to be a problem for most photos. For example, check out the Twitter page shown in Figure 2.7. You see part of a floating dock on the right, and a splash on the left, but the key part of the image (it's a dog in midair after diving off the dock) is blocked by the content area.

For a photo-based background, a better idea is to use a scene where the action isn't just in the middle of the image. A beach shot, landscape, or similar image where the subject either extends across the photo or offers visual interest on the edges is a good way to go. Figure 2.8 shows an example.

2.6 On a typical screen, you only get a bit of room around your content to show off a background image.

The second challenge you face when choosing a background is the size of the image you select. If you use a relatively small image, Twitter displays it in the upper-left corner of the screen, and then fills in the rest of the background with your chosen background color. That's not terrible if your background color goes well with your image, but it's not optimum, either. Twitter does offer an option to tile the background, but few photos look good when tiled.

2.7 If you use a background photo where the subject is in the middle, the subject gets blocked by the Twitter content box.

2.8 A Twitter background where the existence of the content box doesn't spoil the effect

To work around this problem, you should use a relatively large background image, and by "relatively large" I mean a photo with dimensions that are larger than the browser window. This means the background color never appears, and you don't have to worry about tiling the image. Of course, this leads to yet another problem: How large? According to the firm Market Search (see http://marketshare.hitslink.com/report.aspx?qprid=17), as of March 2010 the percentage of users running their screens at various display resolutions broke down as shown in Table 2.1.

Table 2.1 Display Resolution Percentages

Resolution	Percentage of Users
1024 × 768	25.73%
1280 × 800	19.34%
1280 × 1024	10.37%
1440 × 900	8.73%
1680 × 1050	5.51%
800 × 600	2.8%
Other	27.52%

As you can see, the most popular resolution is 1024 × 768, but nearly 30 percent of users run their screens at 1280 pixels wide. So if you assume a maximum width of 1280 pixels, then you have about 75 percent of the market covered (because about 11 percent of those in the "Other" category are running at widths less than 1280 pixels). This means that you should resize your photo to a width of at least 1280 pixels. If you want to cover 90 percent of the market, make your background at least 1440 pixels wide; to get 97 percent coverage, make the image at least 1680 pixels wide. What if you don't want anyone to see the background color? Then you need to use a width of 2560 pixels, which is about the widest screen that anyone runs nowadays.

What about height? Again, you want to make sure that your photo's height is greater than the display height of most of your users. Assuming about 100 vertical pixels are used by the browser (title bar, address bar, and so on), you can see from Table 2.1 that if your photo's height is at least 950 pixels, then you'll cover almost everyone. Again, if you want to be sure that no one sees your background color, go with a height of 1500 pixels (because the maximum screen height these days is 1600 pixels).

You may be wondering how a 950-pixel-high image will work when your profile extends down the page with your tweets. The secret here is that Twitter displays your background image with fixed positioning, so the content area scrolls as you scroll the browser window, but the background remains in place. So as long as the photo is taller than the browser window, no background color appears at the bottom of the screen.

Using a background image to tell people more about yourself

The one-line bio that Twitter includes as part of your profile is limited to a relatively pathetic 160 characters. My life certainly can't be summarized in such a teensy space, and I'm sure yours can't, either. To work around this limitation, many tweeters offer more information about themselves using their profile backgrounds. How? By taking advantage of the gap that most users see to the left of the content box. With a little graphics program know-how, you can create your own background image that includes a picture and some text in a vertical strip that runs down the left side of the image. Make this strip background the same color as your Twitter background, and you've got yourself a nice background and a chance to tell people more about yourself.

How wide should you make this strip? Because most folks use a display resolution of at least 1024 × 768, then almost everyone who visits your Twitter page will see at least a 120-pixel gap to the right of the content box (assuming the browser window is maximized). So make your strip 120 pixels wide, add a nice picture that's the same width, and use your graphics program's text tool to add some text that runs down the strip. Figure 2.9 shows an example (which includes an added design bonus: a 60-pixel-high strip across the top), and Figure 2.10 shows the background applied to a Twitter profile.

The specifics of creating the background image vary depending on the graphics program you use and the tools it offers. One basic procedure is to create a new image that's the height and width you want, and then fill that image with the background color you want. Then use the shape-drawing tool to create a rectangle that's 120 pixels wide and the same height as the background. You can then use the text tool to overlay your text on the rectangle.

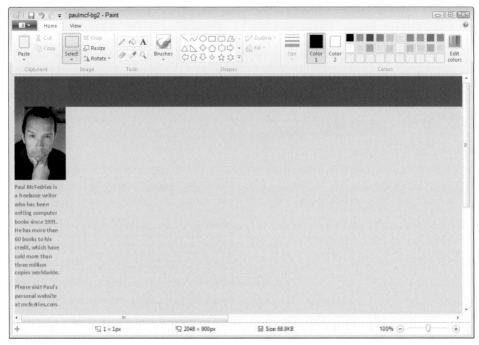

2.9 Create an image with a 120-pixel strip along the left side that includes more info about yourself.

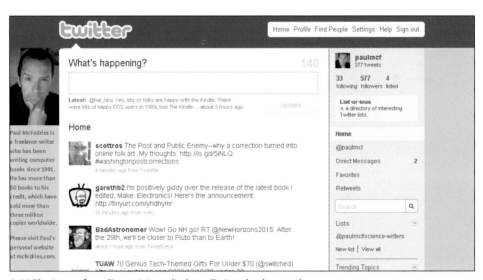

2.10 The image from Figure 2.9 applied as a Twitter background

It's a good idea to test your custom background on a variety of browsers at a variety of display resolutions. If that sounds like way too much work, head over to Browser Shots (http://browsershots.org/) and choose the browsers and screen sizes you want to test.

Overcoming background problems with tiling images

If you really don't want to get into the hassle of worrying about photo sizes, display resolutions, and creating a custom background from scratch, you can get a blissfully problem-free background by applying an image with a pattern that tiles gracefully. Even better, there are plenty of sites out there that either offer ready-made patterns that you can download, or that enable you to generate your own patterns.

For simple pattern downloads, check out the following sites:

- TweetStyle: http://tweetstyle.com
- Twitter Backgrounds Gallery: http://twitterbackgroundsgallery.com
- Twitter Background Images: http://twitterbackgroundimages.com
- TwitBacks: http://twitbacks.com
- Twitr Backgrounds: http://twitrbackground.com
- Twitter Gallery: http://twittergallery.com

If you prefer to come up with your own pattern, here are a few pattern generators you can try out:

- BgPatterns: http://bgpatterns.com
- Colour Lovers: http://colourlovers.com
- Dotted Background Generator: http://pixelknete.de/dotter/
- Stripe Generator: www.stripegenerator.com
- Stripe Mania: http://stripemania.com
- Tartan Maker: www.tartanmaker.com

Choosing Your Profile's Colors

The last bit of design customization you need to perform is to select the colors you want to use for four other aspects of your profile: the text, the links, the sidebar background, and the sidebar border. Here's how it's done:

1. **Sign in to your Twitter account.**

2. **Click Settings.** The Settings page appears.

3. **Click the Design tab.**

4. **Click Change design colors.**

5. **Click the text swatch.** Twitter displays two color controls, as shown in Figure 2.11. The right strip controls the base color, and the left square controls the amount of gray in the color.

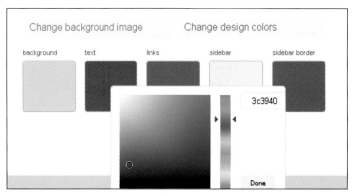

2.11 Click Change design colors, click a color swatch, and then use the color controls to choose the color you want.

6. **Click a spot in the right strip to set the base color.** You can also drag the arrows to set the base.

7. **Click a spot in the left square to set the gray component color.** You can also drag the small circle to set the grayness.

 You can also type a color code directly into the swatch. Use the format rrggbb, where rr is the red component of the color, gg is the green component, and bb is the blue component. Each of these is a two-digit hexadecimal number, where the allowable values run from 00 to 99 and AA to FF.

8. **Repeat Steps 5 to 7 for the links, sidebar, and sidebar border swatches.**

9. **Click Save Changes.** Twitter updates your profile with the new colors.

Stopping Twitter from Sending New Follower Messages

With all these great renovations you've been doing, it won't be long before people start beating a path to your Twitter door. You'll know right away if your custom design is a hit because Twitter sends you an e-mail message every time a kind soul decides to follow you. Personally, I love getting these messages because it's great to know that my tweets have a growing audience, and it also gives me a chance to check out lots of other profiles. You never know who you might come across and decide to follow yourself.

On the other hand, if your profile becomes quite popular, getting tons of messages from Twitter may not appeal to you. Similarly, you might be following as many people as you can handle, so you're not interested in also following any of your new followers.

If that's the case, then you should follow these steps to tell Twitter to stop sending you an e-mail message each time someone follows you:

1. **Sign in to your Twitter account.**
2. **Click Settings.** The Settings page appears.
3. **Click the Notices tab.**
4. **Deselect the New Follower Emails check box.**
5. **Click Save.** Twitter updates your profile with the new setting.

How Do I Send Tweets?

1 2 **3** 4 5 6 7 8 9

Twitter begins with nearly the simplest question you can imagine: What's happening? From that deceptively humble beginning, the entire edifice that is the Twittersphere emerges because it's through these updates — or *tweets* as most Twitterers prefer to call them — that you open up part of your life for other people to see; stay connected with family, friends, and far-flung co-workers; share interesting things you've found online; and learn new things from those intrepid Twitterers who you follow. This chapter introduces you to the surprisingly deep world of the tweet.

Sending a Tweet

There are lots of folks with Twitter accounts who are "read-only" users: They follow others, but they don't post any tweets themselves. That's fine, I guess, if you've simply got nothing to say, but few of us are that tongue-tied. I assume you signed up with Twitter because you've got some things to share, so the next few sections take you through a few ways that you can do just that.

Before we get there, you may be wondering exactly what you should be posting. Are there any rules, official or unofficial, for the type of content that you can send? Fortunately, the answer to that question is a resounding "No!" If what you have to say isn't illegal, then go ahead and say it. Of course, you only have 140 characters to work with, so Twitter is no place for the long-winded. The sheer compactness of a typical Twitter missive means that although the content is as varied as the people who send it, tweets do tend to fall into a few basic categories:

- **Simple status tweets.** These are the purest of the tweets because they're the ones that answer Twitter's original "What are you doing?" query literally. (Twitter changed the question to "What's happening?" in the fall of 2009.) When Twitter began in 2006, this kind of update comprised the vast majority of tweets, but that has been changing recently, and the tweet categories that follow are becoming more prominent as Twitter morphs under the sheer weight of its users.

- **Link to an interesting site.** This is a tweet that provides a short description of some interesting, fun, or useful site, followed by the site's address. (In almost all tweets the addresses have been cut down to size by a URL shortener; see Chapter 9 to learn more.) These types of tweets are becoming increasingly common, and they're a great way to learn new things and to find out about obscure Net nooks that you might otherwise have missed.

- **Link to your own content.** This type of tweet lets your followers know when you've published something elsewhere on the Web. If people like your tweets, then chances are they may also like your blog posts, Flickr albums, or other online content that you create.

- **Conversations.** These tweets are back-and-forth exchanges between two or more people. This is when Twitter becomes very much like an instant messaging system.

- **Broadcasts.** These are tweets with a specific type of content sent on a regular schedule. "Word of the day" (see for example @awad and @thewordoftheday) and "Quotation of the day" (such as @quotesoftheday and @quotations) tweets are good examples.

News. These can be personal "Here's something good (or bad or interesting or whatever) that has happened to me recently" tweets, to the latest news stories sent by professional media organizations.

Live-tweeting. This refers to sending on-the-fly tweets that describe or summarize some ongoing event. The most common live-tweeting scenario is an announcement, speech, or panel discussion at a conference or media event, but live-tweeting is becoming increasingly common at major events, such as the Oscars and the Super Bowl, and breaking news stories, such as the 2008 terrorist attacks in Mumbai, India, and the 2009 Iranian uprising.

Sending a tweet using the Twitter site

There are multiple ways you can post tweets to Twitter, and you learn about most of them elsewhere in the book. However, the most common posting method is still the Twitter site itself, so let's run through the steps:

1. **Sign in to your Twitter account.**

2. **Click Home.**

3. **Use the large What's happening? text box to type your tweet.** As you type, the number above the right edge of the text box counts down from 140 to tell you how many characters you have left. There are three things to note about this countdown:

   - When the count dips below 20, the number color changes to maroon.

   - When the count dips below 10, the number color changes to red.

   - When the count dips below 0, the number color stays red, but it also sprouts a negative sign, and Twitter disables the update button, as shown in Figure 3.1. You need to get the count back to 0 or more before Twitter allows you to post.

4. **Click update. Twitter posts the tweet and adds it to the feed of every person who's following you.**

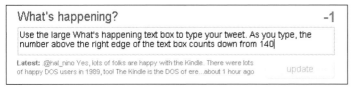

3.1 If you exceed your 140-character allotment, Twitter lets you know by showing a negative number of characters remaining.

Interesting or useful tweets often get *retweeted* — passed along to another person's followers. This is a good thing because it gets your Twitter identity passed around, so consider making your posts retweet friendly. Many people still use the old style of retweet, which consists of the abbreviation RT, followed by *@username* (where *username* is the username of the original tweeter), and then the tweet text. To ensure all this fits inside the retweet, consider making your tweets a maximum of about 120 characters. This is explained in more detail in Chapter 4.

Tips for managing the 140-character limit

If there's one thing that even many nontweeters know about Twitter it's that its messages can be no more than 140 characters long. Why 140 and not, say, 200, or 500, or no limit at all? Twitter was designed originally to use the Short Message Service (SMS) to send out its updates, and on the majority of SMS systems at the time, each message was limited to 160 characters. Twitter's messages had to tack on the username at the front (which can be up to 15 characters long), so it chose 140 characters as the limit for a Twitter update.

Of course, knowing why you've only got 140 characters to express your thoughts is one thing, but actually shoehorning that thought into such a tiny space is quite another. Fortunately, with a bit of practice you'll find yourself getting remarkably adept at crafting 140-words-or-less gems. To help you get there, here are a few pointers to bear in mind when composing your tweets:

- **Take advantage of the symbol short forms that are built in to the language.** Use & or + instead of "and," $ instead of "dollars," % instead of "percent" or "percentage," and so on.

- **Use common abbreviations.** E-mail, chat, instant messaging, and other forms of Internet communication have created a wide variety of abbreviations and acronyms, many of which are in common use: BTW (by the way), FYI (for your information), LOL (laughing out loud), and TTYL (talk to you later). Don't hesitate to use these and other familiar short forms to save characters.

- **Find shorter words.** If there's a key to winning the battle with the 140-character limit, it's this: If a word has a shorter synonym, use the synonym. Delete "perturbed" and replace it with "mad"; get rid of "therefore" and use "so," instead; replace "supercalifragilisticexpialidocious" with "cool."

- **Avoid redundancy and wordiness.** If you're bumping up against the 140-character ceiling, cast a critical eye on your text and ruthlessly rewrite passages that are redundant or that use more words than necessary. For example, use the Delete key to change "in the vicinity of" to "near" and trash "at this point in time" in favor of "now."

● **Be precise.** Twitter is no place to waste words. Your tweets should encapsulate a single thought, idea, action, reaction, or event, and they should discuss that one thing in a way that gets right to the point and says only what needs to be said.

● **Shorten your URLs.** It's not unusual these days for Web addresses to be long-winded affairs that consume dozens of precious characters. To knock a URL down to size, use a URL shortening service such as TinyURL (http://tinyurl.com/), Snurl (http://snurl.com/), or bit.ly (http://bit.ly/). See Chapter 9 to learn more about URL shortening.

Typing nonstandard characters in Twitter

Besides the keys that you can eyeball on your keyboard, you can also include in your tweets a few nonstandard characters, such as € and ™. Twitter supports a character set called UTF-8, which is a list of 400 symbols from the usual alphanumeric suspects to currency symbols, math operators, foreign characters, and more. Table 3.1 presents a few useful characters and their corresponding codes.

Table 3.1 Characters You Can Use In Your Twitter Posts

Character	Code	Character	Code
€	Alt+0128	®	Alt+0174
…	Alt+0133	±	Alt+0177
•	Alt+0149	^{2}	Alt+0178
™	Alt+0153	^{3}	Alt+0179
↓	Alt+0161	¼	Alt+0188
¢	Alt+0162	½	Alt+0189
£	Alt+0163	¾	Alt+0190
¥	Alt+0165	×	Alt+0215
©	Alt+0169	÷	Alt+0247

To type one of these characters, hold down Alt and type the four-digit code using your keyboard's numeric keypad.

Alternatively, use the Character Map application in Windows:

1. **Choose Start ➪ All Programs ➪ Accessories ➪ System Tools ➪ Character Map.** The Character Map window appears.

2. **Double-click the symbol you want to use.** Character Map adds the symbol to the Characters to copy text box.

3. **Click Copy.** Character Map copies the character to the Clipboard.

4. **Switch to your Web browser and position the cursor within the Twitter text box at the position you want the character to appear.**

5. **Press Ctrl+V.** Windows pastes the character into the text box.

Mac fans can use the Character Viewer, which you activate by opening System Preferences, clicking the Language & Text icon, clicking the Input Sources tab, and then selecting the Keyboard & Character Viewer check box. Here are the steps to follow to insert a character:

1. **Click the Keyboard & Character Viewer icon in the menu bar.** Mac OS X displays a menu of commands.

2. **Click Show Character Viewer.** The Characters window appears.

3. **Click the symbol you want to use.**

4. **Switch to your Web browser and position the cursor within the Twitter text box at the position you want the character to appear.**

5. **Click Insert.** Mac OS X pastes the character into the text box.

You can also enter special characters online. Check out a neat tool called TwitterKeys (http://thenextweb.com/TwitterKeys/keys.php), which offers a pop-up window with nearly 200 useful symbols that you can copy and paste into Twitter's tweet text box.

Notes on tweet etiquette

Twitter is a free-form service that doesn't have a whack of rules to follow, and that lack of regulation is a big part of Twitter's appeal for many people. However, that doesn't mean that anything goes on Twitter. Like other forms of online communication, Twitter has evolved a loosely defined set of guidelines that together form a kind of Twitter etiquette (which, inevitably, some folks refer to as *Twittiquette*). There's no definitive list of these do's and don'ts, but some common etiquette ideas have emerged over the past few years. For posting tweets, here are a few etiquette guidelines to consider:

- **Don't send spam.** Nobody wants to see a sales pitch in his or her timeline, so avoid tweets that market products or services. It's certainly okay to tell your followers that you've got a new book, CD, or whatever available, just don't beg people to buy it.

- **Don't overtweet about your other content.** It's perfectly acceptable to let your followers know when you've put content up on some other site, such as your blog. However, if that's all you do, then people will stop following you. Make sure you use Twitter to post original material.

- **Do give credit.** If another person's tweet leads you to find something interesting and you then share that interesting tidbit with your followers, be sure to give a tip of the hat to the original poster. This doesn't have to be anything elaborate. Somewhere in your tweet, just add "via *@username*" or "thanks *@username*," where *username* is the account name of the original tweeter.

- **Don't post private information.** Never include phone numbers, addresses, or other private data (yours or someone else's) in a tweet. Remember that all your tweets appear, albeit briefly, on Twitter's public timeline, which means that anyone, anywhere in the world can see what you post.

- **Don't overshare.** Some folks get so excited about Twitter that they seem to post every thought that pops into their heads. Not only are even your closest friends and family members unlikely to read so many tweets but, even worse, a large number of tweets in a short period of time pushes other people's tweets off each of your followers' personal timelines, and that's just rude.

- **Do treat your fellow tweeters with respect.** Twitter has a fun and relaxed vibe that mostly stems from the respect that most tweeters show each other, and so rude exchanges between users are rare. Do your part to keep Twitter beautiful by keeping your tweets civil and respectful.

Adding hashtags to create a tweet topic

A stream of incoming tweets is typically a real mishmash of people, personalities, and topics, and that's part of the fun and excitement of Twitter. However, every now and then you get a series of tweets centered on a particular topic. It might be an ongoing event, a TV show or movie, or a broader cultural idea such as New Year's resolutions. If you're seeing lots of tweets on a particular subject from your friends, then it's likely that all kinds of other tweeters are talking about the same topic. That means there's likely to be tons of great information about the subject floating around the Twittersphere. That's great, but how do you get your mitts on that info?

You could use the Twitter search engine to track down the relevant tweets, but Twitter offers a much easier method: hashtags. A *hashtag* is a keyword (preceded by the hash symbol — # — hence the name) associated with a particular subject, and tweeters include the hashtag in any tweet on that subject.

For example, as I write this the United Nations Climate Change Conference is happening in Copenhagen, Denmark, and one of the hashtags for that event is #copenhagen. So if someone posts a tweet about the conference, he or she should include the hashtag #copenhagen somewhere in the tweet. This serves to tag the tweet as conference related, so anyone looking for conference tweets needs only to use the Twitter search engine to look for that hashtag, as shown in Figure 3.2.

3.2 To see the recent tweets on a particular topic, type the topic's hashtag into the Twitter Search box and press Enter.

Note that I said that *one* of the hashtags for the conference is #copenhagen. Another is #cop15, which refers to the Fifteenth Conference of the Parties, another name for the climate change conference. For large events, you may need to do some research to ensure you're using the most common hashtag. See Chapter 6 to learn how to search for hashtags. Also, check out Twopular (http://twopular.com) to see which hashtags are currently popular.

Working with Your Tweets

Once you've begun posting tweets in earnest, you may find that you need to perform a little maintenance work from time to time. Twitter doesn't offer many options in this department, but there are three things you can do: delete a tweet, mark a tweet as a favorite, and make your tweets private. The next three sections take you through the details.

Deleting a tweet

One of the unusual and occasionally frustrating quirks of Twitter is that your tweets aren't editable. Once you click the update button, your post gets shipped out to all your friends and what they see is what you sent. If you misspelled a word, made some egregious grammatical gaffe, or forgot to include an address or some other crucial bit of data, too bad; the flawed tweet remains in the Twittersphere for all to see.

When they make a major mistake in a tweet, most tweeters simply send a fresh copy of the tweet with the corrections made (and, if possible, a brief note about what was corrected). Still, that error-filled tweet remains in the timeline. What to do? The one thing that Twitter does allow you to do is delete a tweet. This removes the tweet not only from your profile page (which lists all your tweets), but also from the timelines of everyone who follows you.

Here are the steps to follow to delete a tweet:

1. **Sign in to your Twitter account.**

2. **Click Profile.** Twitter displays a list of your recent tweets.

3. **If you don't see the tweet you want to remove, scroll down to the bottom of the page and click More.** Repeat this until you find the tweet.

4. **Move the mouse pointer over the tweet text.** As you can see in Figure 3.3, the Delete this Tweet icon (a garbage can) appears to the right of the tweet.

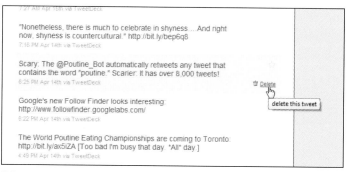

3.3 Hover the mouse over a tweet's text to see the Delete this Tweet icon.

5. **Click the Delete this Tweet icon.** Twitter asks you to confirm the deletion.

6. **Click OK.** Twitter removes the tweet from your profile page as well as from the home pages of all of your followers.

A deleted tweet is gone for good, and no amount of crying, caterwauling, or calls to Twitter tech support will get it back. Double-, no, *triple-check* that you want to blow away the tweet before confirming the deletion.

Adding a tweet to your favorites

Twitter saves copies of all your tweets on your profile page. The most recent 20 tweets appear on the main profile page (log in to your account and click Profile). To see earlier tweets, click the More link at the bottom of the page, and then you keep clicking More to go further back in your tweet history.

This is fine if you only check out your previous tweets from time to time. However, you might occasionally post a tweet that contains something really useful that you want to access frequently, such as a Web site or a quotation. In that case, it can be a real pain to always have to dig back through your tweets to find the tweet you're looking for. To work around this problem, Twitter lets you save that tweet as a favorite, and you can access it quickly by clicking the Favorites link that appears on both your home page and your profile page.

Here are the steps required to save one of your tweets as a favorite:

1. **Sign in to your Twitter account.**

2. **Click Profile.** Twitter displays a list of your recent tweets.

3. **If you don't see the tweet you want to save as a favorite, scroll down to the bottom of the page and click More.** Repeat this until you find the tweet.

4. **Move the mouse pointer over the tweet text.** As you can see in Figure 3.4, the Favorite this Tweet icon (a star) appears to the right of the tweet.

5. **Click the Favorite this Tweet icon.** Twitter adds a copy of the tweet to your Favorites list.

3.4 Hover the mouse over a tweet's text to see the Favorite this Tweet icon.

Twitter also changes the Favorite this Tweet icon to an orange Un-favorite this Tweet icon. As you've no doubt guessed, you click this icon when you no longer want to store a tweet in your Favorites list.

Making your tweets private

A default Twitter account is pretty much an open book:

- Anyone (even people without a Twitter account) can access your home page and view your tweets.
- Each time you post a tweet it appears briefly on Twitter's public timeline for all the world to see.
- Anyone with a Twitter account can follow your tweets.

Most tweeters are fine with this, but you might prefer a less-open approach. If so, you can configure your Twitter account to protect your tweets. This means your account is much more private:

- Only people who follow you can access your home page and view your tweets.
- Your tweets never appear on Twitter's public timeline.
- People who want to follow you must send a request, and you can then either approve or decline that request.

If you like the sound of all that, here are the steps to follow to protect your tweets:

1. **Sign in to your Twitter account.**
2. **Click Settings.** The Settings page appears.
3. **Click the Account tab.**
4. **Select the Protect My Tweets check box.**
5. **Click Save.** Twitter tweets your profile to protect your tweets.

Now when a nonfollower tries to access your Twitter home page, he or she sees the message shown in Figure 3.5.

Twitter also sends you an e-mail message letting you know you have a follower request. That message includes a link that you can click to accept or decline the request. If you want to turn this e-mail option off, see Chapter 2.

3.5 With your Twitter account protected, nonfollowers see this message instead of your tweets.

If that person wants to follow you, he or she must click the Send request button. When that happens, you see a 1 new follower request! message in your home page sidebar, as shown in Figure 3.6. Click that link and then click either Accept or Decline.

Downloading All Your Tweets

Your Twitter tweets appear in your profile pages, so you always have access to all your tweets. However, after you post a few dozen tweets or more, it's a hassle to slog through a bunch of different pages in your profile to find the post you want. You can use the Twitter search engine (see Chapter 6) to track down the post, but that's a bit of a hassle.

3.6 When your Twitter account is protected, you can approve or deny follower requests.

The other problem with having the posts stored in your profile pages is that although this serves as a rough-and-ready backup, do you *really* trust Twitter to keep your tweets safe?

If you want easier access to your tweets, and you want to preserve a local backup copy of your tweets, then you need to download your tweets to your computer. You can do this right from your Web browser by typing a special address that uses the following general syntax:

http://twitter.com/statuses/user_timeline/*account.xml*?count=*n*

Here, replace *account* with your Twitter username, and replace *n* with the number of tweets you want to return. If you want to return all your tweets, log in to your account, check your total number of tweets (it's available on both your home page and your profile page), and then plug that number into the above address as the count value.

What you get in return is a page chock full of data in the XML (extensible markup language) format, as shown in Figure 3.7.

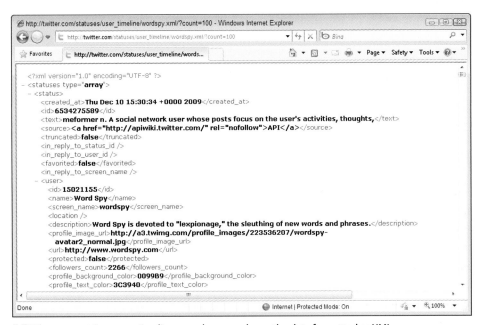

3.7 When you retrieve your timeline, your browser shows the data formatted as XML.

If you'd prefer to receive your tweets in the slightly more friendly comma-separated values (CSV) file format, check out Tweet Scan (www.tweetscan.com), which offers a download feature. It requires you to type your Twitter username and password, but it's safe because it doesn't store your data.

45

Now you save the data by choosing File ➪ Save As, choosing a location and filename in the Save As dialog box, and then clicking Save.

If you have Excel 2007 or later, you can import the XML file into a worksheet for easier viewing, searching, and so on. Here's how:

1. **In Excel, click the Data tab.**

2. **In the Get External Data group, choose From Other Data Sources ➪ From XML Data Import.** The Select Data Source dialog box appears.

3. **Navigate to the XML file location, click the file, and then click Open.** Excel tells you it will create a scheme for the file.

4. **Click OK.** Excel prompts you for a location to import the data.

5. **Click the cell where you want the data to appear, and then click OK.** Excel displays the XML data in a table.

6. **Choose File ➪ Save As, and then use the Save As dialog box to save the data as an Excel workbook.** Consider using the Save as Type list to choose the Excel 97-2003 file format for maximum compatibility. Figure 3.8 shows just such a file loaded into Excel 2010.

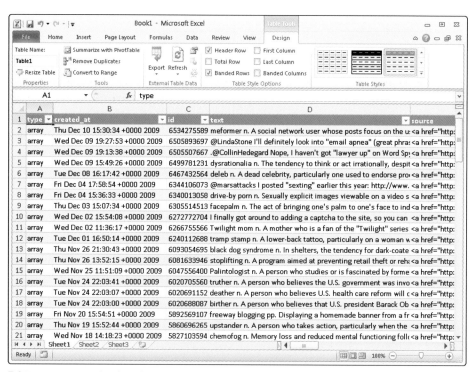

3.8 You can import the downloaded XML file into Excel for easier viewing and searching.

Downloading your tweets is easy, but this method suffers from a glaring problem: As soon as you start posting tweets again, your backup becomes out of date, so you need to perform regular downloads. However, it doesn't make sense to download all your tweets each time. You could adjust the count value based on the number of tweets you've sent since the last download, but Twitter offers an easier way. If you examine Figure 3.7 (and Figure 3.8), you see that each tweet is given a unique ID value. You can use the value to download just those tweets you've posted since your last download. You do that by using your Web browser to enter a special address that uses the following general syntax:

http://twitter.com/statuses/user_timeline/*account*.xml?since_id=*ID*

Again, *account* is your Twitter username, and *ID* is the ID value for the latest tweet in the previous download. For example, in Figures 3.7 and 3.8, you can see that the latest tweet in my @wordspy account has the ID value of 6534275589, so I could download every tweet since that post by using the following address:

http://twitter.com/statuses/user_timeline/wordspy.xml?since_id=6534275589

Working with Mentions and Direct Messages Sent to You

Although at first it looks like Twitter is a one-way medium — you fire off your tweets and that's the end of it — it probably won't take long before you realize that's decidedly not the case. Twitterers are a garrulous bunch, and they don't hesitate to chime in with their couple of cents' worth. They do that either by replying to one of your tweets, or by sending you a direct message. The next few sections show you how to handle the replies and direct messages that come your way.

Viewing tweets that mention you

If another tweeter comes across one of your updates and that person has a response, a retort, or a rebuttal (or simply wants to congratulate you on your wisdom and insight!), he crafts a reply. (You learn how to do this yourself in Chapter 4.) Similarly, a tweeter might include your Twitter name (preceded, as usual, by @) somewhere in an update (such as acknowledging you as the originator of an idea).

Whether they're replies to existing tweets or just updates that include your account name, Twitter calls these *mentions* because they all mention you in some way. Each mention appears on the sender's personal timeline, but your timeline remains resolutely unaffected (unless you're following the tweeter). So how do you see tweets that mention you? By following these steps:

1. **Sign in to your Twitter account.**

2. **Click Home.**

3. **In the sidebar, click @_account_, where _account_ is your Twitter account name.** Twitter displays a list of all the tweets that have mentioned you, as shown in Figure 3.9.

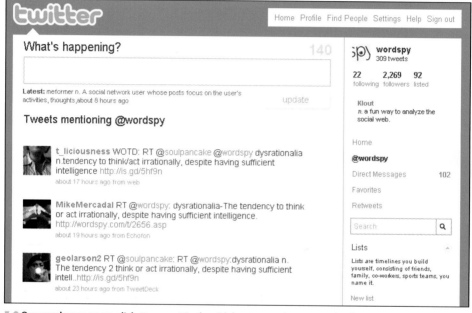

3.9 On your home page, click @_account_ in the sidebar to see the tweets that have mentioned you.

Viewing direct messages sent to you

If you're in a _mutual follow_ Twitter relationship — that is, a person follows you and you also follow that person — then that person can send you a _direct message_, which is a private note that only you see. (Many tweeters refer to direct messages as _directs_.) That is, the direct message doesn't appear on your timeline, so you must follow these steps to read it:

1. **Sign in to your Twitter account.**

2. **Click Home.**

3. **In the sidebar, click Direct Messages.**

4. **Click the Inbox tab.** Twitter displays a list of all the direct messages you've received, as shown in Figure 3.10.

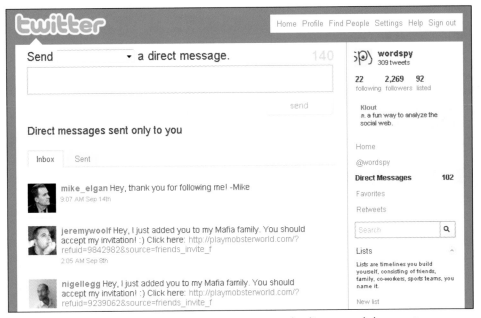

3.10 In your home page sidebar, click Direct Messages to see the directs people have sent you.

Getting an e-mail when you receive a direct message

If someone you're following replies to one of your tweets, then you see that reply in your friend timeline, but for all other replies you must open the @Replies section of your home page. However, direct messages never appear in your timeline, so you must sign in to Twitter to see them. That's a hassle, but luckily it's possible to configure your Twitter account to forward direct messages to your e-mail address. This option is turned on by default in new Twitter accounts, but it's worth following these steps to make sure:

1. **Sign in to your Twitter account.**
2. **Click Settings.**
3. **Click the Notices tab.**
4. **Select the Direct Text Emails check box.**
5. **Click Save.** Twitter updates your account with the new setting.

How Do I follow Other Twitter Users?

1 2 3 4 5 6 7 8 9

Twitter would be just another lonely outpost on the fringes of the Web if all anyone ever did was post tweets. Twitter is, instead, a vibrant, noisy place because it goes beyond mere microblogging and embraces its social side by letting you follow other tweeters. This means that you subscribe to that person's updates, which then appear on your home page, so you can easily keep track of what that person shares with the Twitterverse. By following your pals, family, colleagues, and even total strangers who you find inexplicably fascinating, and by replying to tweets, exchanging messages with your friends, and sending friends' tweets to your followers, you begin to get the full Twitter experience.

Finding People

As you see a bit later, to follow someone on Twitter, you must usually access that person's Twitter page. That's fine and all, but how do you find someone's page? If you don't know anyone on Twitter (or, probably more accurately, if you haven't yet discovered people you know on Twitter), how do you find someone to follow? Fortunately, Twitter offers features that make it fairly easy to find people you know or people who are worth following. The next few sections provide the details.

Finding people with Twitter accounts

The best way to get started is to use the Find on Twitter feature, which enables you to scour the database of tweeters for someone you know. You can search by first name, last name, or even the person's Twitter username. Here's how it works:

1. **Sign in to your Twitter account.**

2. **Click Find People.** The Find People page appears.

3. **Click the Find On Twitter tab.**

4. **Use the text box to type the name (first or last or both) of the person you're looking for.** Using both first and last names is usually the way to go here. If that doesn't work, use just the last name or the first name, whichever is more unique. If all you have is a partial username, you can type that instead.

5. **In the search results, click the person's avatar or username to check out his or her profile.**

Finding someone on another network

Searching for the members of your posse individually using the Find on Twitter feature is an easy way to get going, but it can be time consuming and frustrating if you keep coming up empty. An often better way to go is to get Twitter to do some of the legwork for you. Specifically, you can tell Twitter to rummage through your list of contacts on your Gmail, Yahoo!, or AOL account. If Twitter finds one or more tweeters, it displays them in a list.

Follow these steps to give this a whirl:

1. **Sign in to your Twitter account.**

2. **Click Find People.** The Find People page appears.

3. **Click the Find Friends tab.**

4. **Click the network you want to scour: Gmail, Yahoo, or AOL.**

5. **Type the e-mail address and password for that account, as shown in Figure 4.1.**

If you feel a bit queasy at the thought of handing over your account credentials to Twitter, then good for you for having some security common sense. Many social-networking services offer a similar feature, and you should never dole out third-party login data willy-nilly. Check the site's privacy policy, and only provide your credentials if you trust the site. (Yes, you can trust Twitter.)

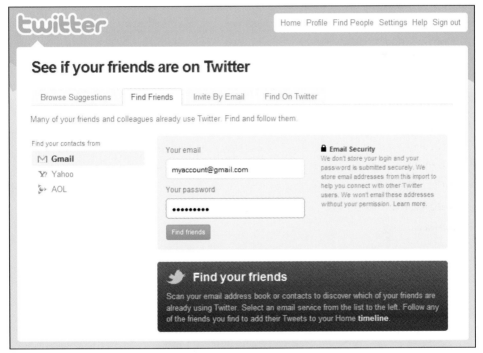

4.1 Choose your network and then type your login credentials.

6. **Click Find friends.** Twitter connects to your account, downloads your contacts list, and then checks for matches in the Twitter database. If it finds any, it displays them in a list.

7. **For each person you want to follow, click Send Request.** Alternatively, click the Follow All *X* button (where *X* is the number of people found) to follow everyone.

8. **To invite non-Twitter friends, click the See Who and Invite Them link.** Twitter displays the Invite Your Friends Who Aren't on Twitter page, which lists all your contacts who don't have a Twitter account. You can use this list to extend invitations to one or more contacts to join Twitter.

9. **Select the check box beside each person you want to invite.**

10. **Click Invite these Contacts.** Twitter fires off an e-mail message to each person.

Inviting someone to join Twitter

Many people enjoy Twitter so much that they want to share the experience with their close friends, respected co-workers, and the saner members of their family. Other tweeters have a hard time finding anyone they know on Twitter, so it becomes a bit of a lonely place. Whichever camp you find yourself in, you can share Twitter with people you know by sending them an e-mail invitation to join the service. The message that Twitter sends on your behalf looks like this:

```
From: Your Name Here
Subject: Your Name Here wants to keep up with you on Twitter
To find out more about Twitter, visit the link below:
http://twitter.com/i/0f6fc06f0d52c55f25246b7316ea81c5324564a6

Thanks,
-The Twitter Team

About Twitter

Twitter is a unique approach to communication and networking based on the
simple concept of status. What's happening? What are your friends
doing—right now? With Twitter, you may answer this question over SMS or
the Web and the responses are shared between contacts.
```

When your friends click the link, they see your Twitter profile page with a link to join up.

If this sounds like a plan, follow these steps to send out the invitations:

1. **Sign in to your Twitter account.**

2. **Click Find People.** The Find People page appears.

3. **Click the Invite By Email tab.**

4. **Use the large text box to type the e-mail address of the person you want to invite.** If you want to fire off multiple invites, separate each address with a comma, as shown in Figure 4.2.

5. **Click Invite.** Twitter dispatches an e-mail message to each address.

---

twitter

Find accounts and follow them.

Browse Suggestions   Find Friends   **Invite By Email**   Find On Twitter

You can invite folks by sending them an email. See what you'll send them.

Enter some email addresses:

```
karen@notweetsforme.com, kyra@tweetingnot
.ca, emily@whatsatwitter.com
```

Separate multiple email addresses with commas, ex: joe@twitter.com, jane@twitter.com

Invite

4.2 Type an e-mail address or three (separated by commas) to invite those lucky folk to join you on Twitter.

Tracking FollowFriday recommendations

Following people you know is a big part of Twitter's appeal, and it adds an irresistible personal touch to the service. However, although I'm sure your friends and family are fascinating, it's a vast Twitterverse, and it's teeming with smart, funny, engaging people whose tweets just might improve your day if you followed them. But how on earth do you find these people? The best way is by asking the tweeters you do know for suggestions. Just post an update asking your followers who they recommend, and then check out the resulting tweeters as the responses come in. (In any Twitter post, if you see @ followed by a username, you can click that username to view the person's profile.)

note A more indirect way to canvass your followers is to check out who they follow. On your home or profile page, click the Followers link, click a username, and then click the person's Following link. I've found perhaps a third of the people I follow using this method.

That should get you a few good recommendations, but why stop at just your followers when you can get the entire Twitosphere involved? Well, perhaps not everyone, but at least every tweeter who knows about FollowFridays. This is a Twitter topic where every Friday people post one or more updates that recommend one or more particularly good tweeters. Each update includes the #followfriday hashtag (or sometimes #ff, just to be a pain), so all FollowFridays are easily found and searched. Here are a couple of ways you can track FollowFriday updates:

- **Use Twitter search.** You can use Twitter's advanced search feature to search for a particular hashtag. I talk about this in detail in Chapter 6, but for now you can plug the following address into your Web browser: http://twitter.com/#search?q=followfriday.

- **Use TopFollowFriday.** This site tracks the most endorsed tweeters, either on the current day or all time: http://topfollowfriday.com/.

Following People

The best way to revel in another person's Twitter goodness is to follow that person. Sure, you can simply use your Web browser to dial up a person's Twitter profile and read his or her stuff, but you lose the immediacy of seeing updates arrive in your timeline, and you miss out on some of the social aspects of Twitter (such as not being able to send a message directly to that person).

Following someone on Twitter

Following someone on Twitter usually takes just a single click, but what you click depends on where you are in the Twitter interface. There are two possibilities:

- **Viewing a person's profile page.** In this case, look for the Follow button under the person's avatar. Twitter replaces the Follow button with a Following notice, as shown in Figure 4.3.

- **Viewing a list of followers or friends.** In this case, each tweeter in the list has a Follow button (see Figure 4.4), and you click that button to follow that person. Twitter removes the Follow button and displays Following, as shown in Figure 4.4.

4.3 In a tweeter's profile page, click the Follow link and Twitter changes your status to Following.

note If you see a lock icon beside the person's username, it means the user must approve your follow request because his or her updates are protected. When you click the Follow button, Twitter replaces it with a Pending message.

4.4 In a list of followers or friends, click a tweeter's Follow link and Twitter changes your status, as shown here.

Following Twitter's suggested users

If you're really not sure where to start with this following business, then you might want to take a look at Twitter's Browse Suggestions page, which lists hundreds of Twitter users. That sounds intimidating, I know, but fortunately Twitter is smart enough to organize everything by category: Books, Business, Fashion, Funny, Science, Sports, and more. It's not exactly personal, but it's an easy way to populate your friend timeline.

note To keep track of the most popular tweeters, check out Twitterholic at http://twitterholic.com.

Here are the steps to follow:

1. **Sign in to your Twitter account.**
2. **Click Find People.** The Find People page appears.
3. **Click the Browse Suggestions tab.** Twitter displays a list of categories.
4. **Click a category that interests you.** Twitter displays a list of tweeters in that category (see Figure 4.5).
5. **Click Follow.** Twitter adds the user to your list of friends.
6. **Repeat steps 4 and 5 to bulk up your friends.**

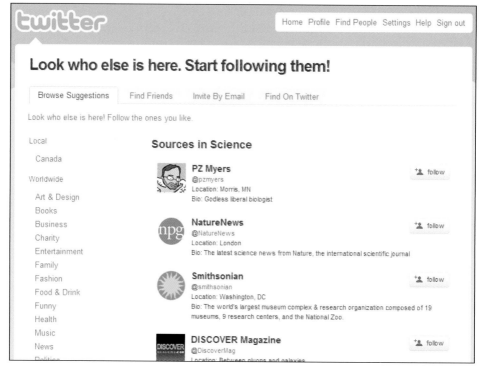

4.5 In the Browse Suggestions tab, select the check box beside each user you want to follow.

Understanding verified accounts

Twitter is home to a remarkable number of celebrities: movie stars, sports bigwigs, technical writers, you name it. For many people, this is one of the most amazing and unique features of Twitter because it seems to give you incredible access to the day-to-day lives of the rich and famous. Unfortunately, Twitter is also home to a remarkable number of *fake* celebrities: accounts that appear to be posting tweets from an honest-to-gosh celeb, but that are actually just the musings of some wannabe in Wilmington.

The problem is that Twitter doesn't ask for ID when you create an account. If you want to use the name of some famous person as your Twitter moniker, there's nothing stopping you, and hundreds of too-much-time-on-their-hands miscreants have done just that. Twitter seemed to more or less turn a blind eye to these ersatz accounts, but then Tony LaRussa, the manager of baseball's St. Louis Cardinals, decided to sue Twitter because an imposter was posting tweets under his name. That caught Twitter's collective attention in a hurry, and the solution it came up with is the so-called *verified account*. Basically, if you sign up for a Twitter account and you're famous enough to have people wanting to impersonate you, then Twitter HQ will jump through a few extra hoops to ensure you are who you say you are.

The upshot for the rest of us is the Verified Account badge that you see at the top of a legit celebrity's sidebar. Figure 4.6 shows an example for the Twitter account of the band Coldplay.

4.6 The fabulously famous now come with a Verified Account badge.

tip If you're famous, or if you're having problems with someone impersonating you on Twitter, you can request that the Twitter folk verify your account. Fill in the Verified Account form at http://twitter.com/account/verify_request. You may not be verified (as I write this Twitter is verifying only a limited number of accounts), but it doesn't hurt to ask.

Following a person's updates via RSS

If you're a dedicated blog follower and find yourself spending more time in your RSS reader than just about anywhere else, you might not like the idea of having to access the Twitter site or even sign in to your Twitter account to follow a particular person's tweets. Similarly, you might be following someone's tweets and you don't want to miss a thing while you're not signed in to Twitter. In both cases, Twitter makes each user's timeline available in an RSS feed so you can add that feed to your favorite RSS reader. Here's how it works:

1. **Sign in to your Twitter account.** Actually, this part is optional because you don't need to be logged in to access someone's RSS feed. However, if you want to get the feed for one of your friends or followers, then you need to sign in.

2. **Navigate to the user's profile page.**

3. **In the sidebar, click the RSS feed of *username*'s tweets link, where *username* is the user's screen name.** Twitter displays the feed.

4. **Subscribe to the feed.** The steps required here vary depending on your RSS reader. The standard technique is to copy the feed URL in the browser's address bar, navigate to your RSS service, select the option to add a feed, and then paste the feed address.

If you want to follow all your friends via RSS, sign in, and then click Home to display your friend timeline. In the sidebar, click the RSS feed link and then type your Twitter login credentials in the dialog box that appears.

Following people who follow you

One of the ongoing debates in Twitter circles involves the question of whether you should always follow someone who follows you. Many tweeters believe that it's rude not to follow someone who has been kind enough to sign up for your tweets. After all, that person has indicated an interest in what you have to say, so by not reciprocating you're effectively saying you're not interested in what that person has to say. Not only that, but Twitter's direct message feature (which I discuss in just a bit) requires that two users follow each other. Believe it or not, many Twitter geeks examine a user's *follow ratio*, which compares the number of people that user follows with the number of people who follow the user. A low follow ratio means that a person follows few people compared to how many follow her, and to many tweeters, that's a bad sign.

Other tweeters counter that Twitter isn't (or shouldn't be) a numbers game. Your friend timeline should be a reflection of your interests, your work life, or your social life (or even all three), and automatically adding tweeters to your list of friends defeats that purpose because you're bound to get deluged with updates you're completely uninterested in, or even offended by. Even worse, if you're lucky enough to become popular on Twitter, do you really want your timeline to be inundated with the tweets from hundreds or even thousands of users, the vast majority of whom you don't know from Adam?

Which side of the fence you come down on in this debate really depends on what you want to get out of Twitter. If you want to keep in touch with friends, family, and a few tweeters that you've found interesting or entertaining, then follow who you want; if you want the complete social experience that Twitter provides, follow everyone who comes your way.

Following someone who is following you

If you decide to go the latter route, then Twitter offers a couple of methods you can use to follow a person who is now following you:

- **E-mail link.** Assuming you've configured Twitter to send you an e-mail message each time someone follows you, display that message in your e-mail program, and then click the link to view the person's profile. When the profile loads in your Web browser, click the Follow button.

⦿ **Twitter site.** Load your home page or profile page, click your follower's link, and then click the Follow button beside the user.

Automatically following someone who follows you

Following your followers manually isn't a big deal if you only receive a few friend requests per day. However, if your Twitter profile takes off, you might become insanely popular and start receiving dozens of new followers each day. That's a nice position to be in, for sure, but you could end up spending vast chunks of your day just processing all those new fans.

To avoid that, you can use a powerful online tool called SocialOomph (formerly TweetLater) to automatically follow anyone who follows you. Go to www.socialoomph.com and sign up for a free registration. (There's a paid version of the service, but you don't need it for this.) After you do that, you add your Twitter account and then configure it to automatically follow your followers. Because SocialOomph is an online service, the interface changes fairly regularly. However, here are the steps to follow to add your Twitter account as I write this:

1. **Log on to your SocialOomph account.**
2. **Click the Accounts tab.**
3. **Click the Add Account tab.** The Add New Account page appears.
4. **Select the Twitter option and click Continue.** The Add a New Twitter Account page appears.
5. **Type your screen name in the Twitter User Name text box.**
6. **Type your password in the Twitter Password text box.**
7. **Type the Bot Prevention text.**
8. **Click Save.** SocialOomph saves your Twitter account info.

You can now activate the Auto Follow feature:

1. **Click the Accounts tab.**
2. **Click the Edit Automation tab.**
3. **Click the Edit link beside your Twitter account.** The Optional Twitter Account Automation page appears.
4. **Select the Auto Follow check box, as shown in Figure 4.7.**
5. **Click Save.** SocialOomph adds your accounts and configures them to automatically follow your followers.

Optional Twitter Account Automation	
Auto Welcome:	☐ Automatically send a welcome message to new followers.
Message Sending Method:	All welcome messages are sent as Direct Messages.
Send This Message:	How to rotate welcome messages (and why you should).
	Best Practise: The message should not be about you, it should be about your follower and your future interaction with your follower. Write a very simple welcome message. If you really want folks to unfollow you, then try and sell them something with this first welcome message. Very few people like that. Be careful even if you're giving away something for free. The purpose of this message is to say hello and welcome. Most people take a dim view of you when you do any kind of self-promotion with this message. If your message smells remotely like, "Hi, thanks for the follow, now buy my stuff or do something that will benefit me or check out how cool I am," then you really are misusing this welcome message. Don't send what you wouldn't like to receive from others.
Auto Follow:	☑ Automatically follow people (new followers) who follow me from this point forward.

4.7 Add your Twitter account to SocialOomph and select the Auto Follow check box.

note As I write this, SocialOomph waits about 8 hours before processing your new followers, and it then checks your account a couple of times a day to look for new followers. SocialOomph does not process your existing followers, so if you want to follow them you must do it manually.

Downloading your friends' tweets

If you're a bit behind on your friends' tweets and you're looking for a way to catch up while you're offline, this usually requires a Twitter client such as the programs I discuss in Chapter 8. However, if you're willing to wrestle with some XML code, then here's another method you can use:

1. **In your Web browser, type the following address, where you replace *n* with the number of updates you want to retrieve:**

   http://twitter.com/statuses/friends_timeline.xml?count=*n*

2. **Press Enter or Return.** The Twitter server prompts you to log on to your account.

3. **Type your Twitter username and password.** The browser displays the updates in XML format. See Chapter 3 to learn how to import an XML file into Excel 2010 or 2007.

There are also many XML viewers available for free. Google "XML viewer" and you'll get lots of hits.

Stop following someone on Twitter

Unfortunately, it's a fact of Twitter life that not everyone is interesting! Some people take the What's happening? question too much to heart, some people are rude, and some people simply overshare. Whatever the reason, if someone's updates are clogging your timeline, it's best to "defriend" that person and stop following them. There are two ways you can do this:

● **Viewing your list of followers.** Sign in to your account, click either Home or Profile, and then click Followers. Locate the person you want to get rid of, click the Actions button (the gear icon) beside that person's info, and then click the Unfollow *username* command, where *username* is the Twitter name of the person you want to remove (Figure 4.8 shows an example).

4.8 Click the user's Actions button and then click the Unfollow command.

● **Viewing a person's profile page.** In this case, click the Actions button and then click the Unfollow *username* command, where *username* is the person's Twitter name.

Twitter doesn't tell you when people quit following you. If you want to know, sign up with Qwitter at http://useqwitter.com/.

Replying, Retweeting, and Direct Messaging

Twitter is a social network, and part of what that entails is the exchange of messages between tweeters. This is mostly achieved by posting tweets that then appear on the friend timelines of the folks who follow you, but Twitter also offers three other ways to create conversations and exchanges: replying to an update, retweeting an update, and sending someone a direct message. The next three sections tackle the specifics.

Replying to a tweet

A *reply* is a response to a tweeter's update, and that response appears on your timeline as well as on the original tweeter's timeline. You usually send replies to people you follow, but on Twitter anyone can send a reply to anyone (as long as that person's account isn't protected). Send a reply when you have a comment about a tweet, you want to follow up on a tweet, or you have new information about a tweet.

Here are the steps to follow to reply to an update:

1. **Sign in to your Twitter account.**

2. **Locate the update to which you want to reply.** The update might appear on your friend timeline, in your mentions timeline, a tweeter's timeline, the Twitter public timeline, or in the result of a Twitter search.

3. **If the update appears in a timeline, hover the mouse pointer over the update.** Twitter displays the Reply link and the Reply to *username* banner (where *username* is the name of the person who posted the tweet; see Figure 4.9). If the update appears in a list of Twitter search results, you see a Reply arrow instead.

4. **Click the Reply link.** If you're working with search results, click the Reply arrow instead. Twitter displays the Reply to *username* text box and adds *@username* to the box (where, in both cases, *username* is the tweeter's screen name).

jonahlehrer The paper makes me wish I was a better at taking naps: http://www.saramednick.com/htmls/pdfs/Cai_PNAS_2009.pdf
about 4 hours ago via web — Reply — Retweet

TUAW That's two! RT @mikepuchol Macnification, reviewed here: http://bit.ly/aj3aPX RT @eugenekhoo MovieGate. http://bit.ly/rSVVy
about 4 hours ago via Tweetie

4.9 Hover the mouse pointer over a tweet to see the Reply link.

5. **Type your reply, as shown in Figure 4.10**.

6. **Click Tweet.** Twitter posts the reply, which then appears in your update timeline as well as in the user's mentions timeline.

Reply to jonahlehrer: 43

@jonahlehrer I'm more of a "sleep camel" kind of guy: http://www.wordspy.com /words/sleepcamel.asp

Latest: Stunning images generated from mathematical equations: http://bit.ly/dw5iOC about 8 hours ago

Tweet

4.10 Type your response in the Reply to *username* text box.

If you can't find the tweet to which you want to reply, don't sweat it because you can still send a reply as long as you know the tweeter's username. Sign in to your account, and then click Home. In the What's happening? text box, type *@username*, where *username* is the tweeter's screen name. When you press spacebar, Twitter changes the text box name to Reply to *username*. Now type your response and click Reply.

Sending a reply to all your followers

When you send a reply (or any tweet that begins with *@username*), the resulting tweet appears in your profile timeline and in the friend timeline of the person you replied to. What about the people you follow? That is, because you normally see their tweets in your friend timeline, do you also see the replies they send out to other people? The answer is that it depends on who they reply to:

⊙ If a person you follow replies to another person you follow, then the reply shows up in your friend timeline.

⊙ If a person you follow replies to a person you don't follow, then the reply does *not* appear in your friend timeline.

This configuration makes sense when you think about it. For example, suppose you follow Kyra and David, and Kyra replies to one of David's tweets. Because you're following both people, then chances are you saw David's tweet that Kyra is replying to, so you probably understand (or can figure out) what she's talking about in her reply. Therefore, it's reasonable for you to see Kyra's reply on your friend timeline.

On the other hand, suppose you follow Kyra but not David. In this case, you won't have seen David's original tweet, so Kyra's reply might be gibberish; it makes sense for the reply to not appear on your friend timeline.

However, there may be times when you want to reply to someone and you want that reply to also be seen by *all* the people who follow you. After all, if your reply contains useful, relevant, or fun info, why shouldn't you share it with all your friends? Twitter offers no feature that handles this kind of scenario directly, but as is often the case with Twitter, the users have come up with their own solution.

The trick uses the fact that if you include a person's *@username* anywhere in the tweet *except* the beginning, then Twitter treats it like a regular update and ships it to all your followers. So, to send a reply that's also seen by all your followers, start the response with a single character such as a dot (.), a tilde (~), or something similarly nonintrusive. Then type the *@username*, followed by your response text. The resulting tweet *looks* like a reply, but all your followers see your wise or witty riposte.

Retweeting an update

A *retweet* is another person's tweet that you send out to your followers. You most often retweet updates from the people you follow, but you're free to retweet anyone's updates. Retweet an update if you think it will be especially interesting or relevant to the people who follow you.

Here are the steps to follow to retweet to an update:

1. **Sign in to your Twitter account.**
2. **Locate the update you want to retweet.** The update might appear on your friend timeline, in your mentions timeline, a tweeter's timeline, or the Twitter public timeline.

You can also retweet any update that you come across using Twitter's search engine (which I talk about in Chapter 6).

3. **Hover the mouse pointer over the update.** Twitter displays the Retweet link.

4. **Click the Retweet link.** Twitter displays a dialog box asking you to confirm that you want to retweet the update to all your followers, as shown in Figure 4.11.

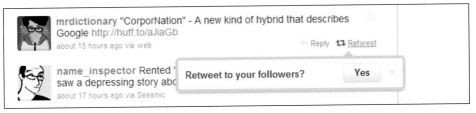

4.11 Click an update's Retweet link to forward it to all your followers.

5. **Click Yes.** Twitter posts the retweet, which then appears in your profile timeline as well as in the timelines of all your followers.

Figure 4.12 shows you what a retweet looks like in a follower's timeline. A few extra tidbits tell you that this is a retweet instead of a regular update:

- The original tweeter's avatar and username appear along with the tweet.

- The original tweeter's username is preceded by the retweet icon.

- The relative time shown with the tweet is the time of the original update, not the retweet.

- You see the message Retweeted by *username* and *x* others, where *username* is the person who retweeted the update, and *x* is the number of other people who have retweeted the same update.

Home

mrdictionary "CorporNation" - A new kind of hybrid that describes Google http://huff.to/aJiaGb

about 15 hours ago via web

Retweeted by **wordspy** and 1 other

4.12 When the retweet shows up in someone's timeline, Twitter adds a few extras so you know it's a retweet and not a regular update.

Happily, the retweet feature is smart enough to know when someone retweets an update that you've already seen. For example, if someone retweets an update from someone you already follow, you'll see the original tweet in your timeline, but you won't see the retweet. Thanks, Twitter!

What I've just described is the "official" Twitter method of retweeting an update. There is, however, an "unofficial" method that's still quite common, so you need to know about it. The *organic* retweet (as the honchos at Twitter headquarters insist on calling it) is a feature that was developed by the Twitter community a while back, and it became a standard part of the tweeter's posting arsenal. An organic retweet is an update that uses the following general form:

```
RT @username: original tweet [your comment]
```

Here, *username* is the name of the original tweeter; *original tweet* is the text of the update you're retweeting; and *your comment* is text that you add to comment on the update. Note, first of all, that this format isn't the only way to retweet. Some folks add their comments to the beginning, some people put the username at the end, while others use "retweet" or "retweeting" instead of RT.

Here's the basic procedure for retweeting an update using the RT method:

1. **Sign in to your Twitter account.**
2. **Locate the update you want to retweet.** The update might appear on your friend timeline, in your mentions timeline, a tweeter's timeline, the Twitter public timeline, or in the result of a Twitter search.
3. **Copy the tweet text, including the username at the beginning of the tweet.**
4. **Click Home.**
5. **Click inside the What's happening? text box.**
6. **Type RT.**
7. **Type a space and then @.**
8. **Paste the text you copied in Step 3.**

9. **Type your own text (if you have room) after the original tweet text.**

10. **Click Update.** Twitter posts the retweet, which then appears in your update timeline.

To keep track of the most popular retweets and the most retweeted users, check out Retweetist at http://retweetist.com.

What if you come across a tweet that contains an interesting idea or a useful link, but you don't want to quote the original tweeter verbatim? For example, you might have your own spin on the original topic and so you want to post your thoughts along with the link. In that case, it's proper Twitter etiquette to acknowledge the original tweeter by including somewhere in your update the text "via @*username*," where *username* is the screen name of the original tweeter.

So, I hear you asking, are you supposed to use the official Twitter retweet feature or the organic RT method? The answer is that it depends:

- Use the official retweet method if you don't want to add a comment to the retweet, or if the original retweet is so long that it won't fit into an RT update without serious editing.

- Use the old-fashioned RT method if you want to include your two cents' worth when you retweet.

Viewing your retweets

By definition, retweets are updates that you found fascinating enough or funny enough to pass along to your posse. So it stands to reason that you might want to check out a particular retweet later on to relive the moment. If you used the official Twitter retweet method, you're in luck because Twitter keeps track of your retweets. Here's how to get at them:

1. **Sign in to your Twitter account.**

2. **Click Home.**

3. **In the sidebar, click Retweets.** Twitter takes you to the retweets page.

4. **Click the Retweets By You tab.** Twitter displays a list of your retweets, as shown in Figure 4.13.

4.13 Click the Retweets By You tab to see your retweets.

Sending a direct message to someone

A *direct message* is a note that you send directly to a tweeter, where "direct" means that the message doesn't appear on either your timeline or the recipient's timeline. You can only send a direct message to someone if the two of you follow each other. Send a direct message when you want a private exchange with someone.

How you send a direct message depends on where you are in the Twitter landscape:

● If you're viewing the list of people you follow, click the Actions button and then click Direct Message *username*, where *username* is the person you want to contact.

● If you're on the profile page of a mutual follower, click the Actions button and then click Direct Message *username*.

● If you're viewing your Direct Messages timeline (click Home, click Direct Messages in the sidebar, and then click the Sent tab), use the Send *x* a direct message list to choose your recipient (see Figure 4.14).

Whichever message you use, Twitter displays a text box. Type your message in the box, as shown in Figure 4.14, and then click send.

4.14 After you choose your recipient, type the message and click send.

If you're having a hard time finding the person you want to direct-message, you don't need to use the Twitter interface to find him or her. If you know the person's username, you can click Home and use the What are you doing? text box to type a message that uses the following general format:

d *username message*

Here, *username* is the screen name of the person you want to write to, and *message* is your text. When your message is ready, click Send to ship it.

Finally, if someone sends you a direct message, you might feel like writing back. The easiest way to do this is through your Direct Messages Inbox (click Home, click Direct Messages in the sidebar, and then click Inbox). Hover the mouse over the message you want to respond to; then click the Reply link. Type your response in the text box and then click Tweet.

note   To keep your Direct Messages timeline less cluttered, delete any messages you no longer need. Hover the mouse pointer over the message, and then click the Delete link. When Twitter asks you to confirm the deletion, click OK.

Configuring direct message e-mails

When you follow someone and that person also follows you, the two of you can send direct messages to each other. Because direct messages are more personal, Twitter automatically configures your account to send any direct messages you receive to your e-mail address. If you want to turn off this feature, or if you like the idea and want to make sure this setting is activated, follow these steps:

1. **Sign in to your Twitter account.**

2. **Click Settings.** Your Twitter account settings appear.

3. **Click the Notices tab.**

4. **To get direct messages via e-mail, select the Direct Text Emails check box.**

5. **Click Save.** Twitter configures your account with the new setting.

Working with the People You Follow

Once you start following people on Twitter, your interactions with them will mostly consist of reading their tweets, replying when you've got something to say, and sending direct messages to people who also follow you. However, Twitter does offer a few other choices, such as displaying a person's updates and retweets, as well as blocking a user. The next few sections provide the details.

Checking out a person's updates

If you follow a bunch of people, a particular update from a particular user can fall off the first page of your friend timeline in a hurry. Rather than slogging through your timeline pages to locate the tweet, it's often easier to display the person's updates. This is also useful if you've been offline (or just off-Twitter) for a while and you want to catch up with a favorite friend.

Twitter gives you several ways to access a user's tweet timeline, depending on where you are in the interface:

- If you see an update from that person in your friend timeline, click the username at the start of the tweet.

- If you've got the person on-screen in your list of followers, click the username.

- Use your Web browser to type http://twitter.com/*username*, where *username* is the Twitter screen name of the person you want to read.

Preventing a person's retweets from appearing in your timeline

Earlier you learned how to send a retweet the official Twitter way by clicking the Retweet link beside an update. This is a great way to share tweet gold with your followers. Hopefully, some of your friends are also retweeting because it's one of the best ways to find interesting Twitterers. However, in the world of retweets there's sharing and then there's *over*sharing. Some folks seem to think that nine out of every ten tweets they receive are retweet-worthy, so your regular friend timeline gets inundated with a bunch of recycled (and usually uninteresting) updates.

If a particular Twitterer's retweet habit is sticking in your craw, help is just around the corner. Twitter offers a setting that enables you to block all the retweets sent by someone you follow. (Note that this setting only works with official retweets; the old-fashioned RT-style retweets aren't affected.) Here are the steps to follow to block someone's retweets:

1. **Sign in to your Twitter account.**

2. **Navigate to the home page of the person whose retweets you want to block.** You can do this either by clicking the Following link in your sidebar and then clicking the user's name, or by navigating directly to twitter.com/*username*. When you get to the user's page, look for the Retweet icon to the right of the Following indicator.

3. **Click the Retweet icon.** The icon turns from green to white to indicate that you will no longer receive that person's retweets. To make sure, hover the mouse pointer over the icon as shown in Figure 4.15.

4.15 Click the Retweet icon to prevent someone you follow from infesting your friend timeline with retweets.

Viewing your friends' retweets

As I mentioned before, when someone you follow retweets an update, that retweet shows up in your friend timeline. And, of course, just like a regular update, that retweet slowly (or sometimes quickly) gets buried under the incessant accumulation of new tweets. Because retweets are quite often interesting or useful, wouldn't it be nice if there were some easy way to locate a retweet later on?

As I also mentioned before, a retweet doesn't appear in your friend timeline if you've already seen the update (because the original was posted by someone you follow). That prevents you from having to wade through duplicate tweets, but sometimes it's useful to know that one of your friends' updates is being retweeted hither and thither. Wouldn't it be nice if there was some easy way to see these hidden retweets?

I also told you earlier that when you see a retweet in your timeline, the update says Retweeted by *username* and *x* others, where *username* is the name of the retweeter, and *x* is the number of times the original update has been through the retweet mill. Wouldn't it be nice if there were some easy way to find out who else has retweeted the update?

Fortunately, the answer to each of the three not-so-musical questions posed in the previous three paragraphs is "Yes!" Twitter maintains a complete list of all the updates that people you follow have retweeted. This list includes not only the retweets that you saw in your timeline, but also the hidden retweets where you saw the originals. The list also shows you the avatars of each person who has retweeted the update. Here's how to see this list:

1. **Sign in to your Twitter account.**

2. **Click Home.**

3. **In the sidebar, click Retweets.** Twitter takes you to the retweets page.

4. **Click the Retweets by others tab.** Twitter displays a list of your friends' retweets, as shown in Figure 4.16.

4.16 Click the Retweets by others tab to see all the retweets that have been shipped out by the folks you follow.

Viewing your tweets that have been retweeted

There aren't many chances in life to get our egos stroked, even for a short time, but Twitter can help because you get a nice little ego boost every time some kind soul retweets one of your updates. For an even bigger shot of self-esteem, check out the complete list of your updates that have been retweeted:

1. **Sign in to your Twitter account.**

2. **Click Home.**

3. **In the sidebar, click Retweets.** Twitter takes you to the Retweets page.

4. **Click the Your tweets, retweeted tab.** Twitter displays a list of all your updates that have been retweeted, as shown in Figure 4.17.

4.17 Click the Your tweets, retweeted tab to see your updates that have been retweeted.

Blocking a tweeter

A huge number of people use Twitter, and most of those folks seem to get the friendly Twitter vibe. Of course, anytime you're dealing with a massive crowd you're bound to come across a bad apple or three. It might be someone who's rude or offensive, a huckster using Twitter to sell snake oil, or a company that bombards you with marketing messages. In most cases, the easiest solution is to stop following the user and, if the user is also following you, to remove the person from your list of followers.

That usually works, but there's a small subset of pests who'll just start following you all over again, or who'll send you replies even if they're not following you. For these hard-core cases, Twitter offers a hard-core solution: Block the user. Blocking someone means that he or she can't follow you and can't send you replies.

Twitter gives you two ways to block a user:

- If the person is currently following you, open your list of followers, click the person's Actions button, and then click the Block *username*.

- If the person isn't following you, go to his or her profile page and click the Actions button, and then click Block *username*, as shown in Figure 4.18.

4.18 To shut annoying tweeters out of your life, access their profile page, click Actions, and then click Block *username*.

Taking Advantage of Twitter Lists

Your friend timeline shows all the tweets posted by everyone you follow, which if you think about it, is a bit odd. After all, you don't usually socialize with your friends, family, and co-workers at the same time, so why should you social-network with all three groups at the same time? Separating your social cohorts is fairly easy offline, but it's not so easy on Twitter. Yes, you could set up a different Twitter account for each social group, but that's just adding several layers of complexity to your online life.

A much better solution is to take advantage of Twitter lists. A list is just a collection of Twitter users who are related in some way. For example, there's a list that consists of all the people who work for Twitter, another for the reporters who contribute to the *New York Times*' Bits blog, and yet another for the funniest people on Twitter (in one person's opinion, anyway). In fact, there are thousands of lists in dozens of categories including technology, the arts, journalism, sports, celebrities, and politics. Best of all, you can create your own lists, which enables you to separate your friends from your family, your colleagues from your co-dependents.

Following a list

A list is a kind of subaccount on Twitter. That is, every list is created and maintained (or *curated* in the vernacular) by a Twitter user and, just as you don't see regular updates from a tweeter until you follow that user, you don't see regular updates from a list until you follow that list. What do I mean by "regular updates from a list"? Just that the list generates its own timeline that shows every tweet from every user on the list. Note that, crucially, this is a *separate* timeline. That is, once you follow a list, the tweets generated by the list do *not* appear in your regular friend timeline.

As I said, lists are created and curated by Twitter users, so you follow a list by going to the user's home page. Here's how it works:

1. **Sign in to your Twitter account.**

2. **Navigate to the user's home page.** In the sidebar, you see a Lists section, which is, as you might guess, a list of the user's lists. Figure 4.19 shows an example. Notice that all list names have the format *@username/listname*, where *username* is the user who curates the list, and *listname* is the name of the list.

3. **If you don't see the list you want, click View all to see the user's complete collection.** Twitter takes you to the retweets page.

Lists

@jayrosen_nyu/twitter-s-best-stylists

@jayrosen_nyu/studio-20-people

@jayrosen_nyu/best-mindcasters-i-know

@jayrosen_nyu/top-journalism-linkers

@jayrosen_nyu/young-smart-newsies

View all

4.19 In the user's sidebar, the Lists section tells you the lists that the user curates.

4. **Click the list you want to follow.** Twitter displays the list home page (see Figure 4.20 for an example), which shows a description of the list, the current list timeline, and some list stats. (Following tells you the number of tweeters on the list; Followers tells you the number of people who follow the list.)

5. **Click Follow this list.** Twitter adds you as a list follower, and the list name now appears in your home page sidebar in the Lists section. To view the list's timeline, click the list in your sidebar.

I know, I know: it's easy for me to tell you to navigate to some user's home page to follow one of that person's lists, but how in the name of (Twitter co-founder) Biz Stone are you supposed to know who has lists that you can follow? By far the best way to become list-savvy on Twitter is to make tracks to a site called Listorious (http://listorious.com/). This site organizes lists by category, shows you the most-followed lists, has a search feature, and much more.

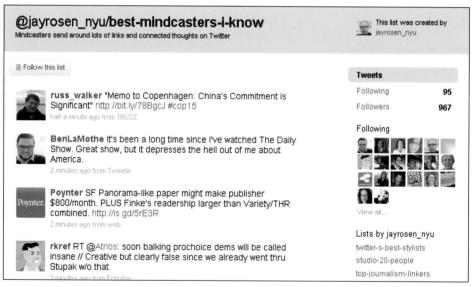

4.20 The home page for a typical Twitter list

Creating a list

Twitter lists are good, clean fun, and possibly even addictive. You'll know when the list bug has infected your digital bloodstream when you get the urge to create your own list. Why the heck not, because making a list of one's own is easy and free, and it gives you a chance to get creative with the Twitterverse? Yes, you can create standard lists for friends, family, and co-workers, but why stop there? Twitter is home to an amazing variety of people, so your lists can reflect that: Cubic Zirconia Experts; Malibu Barbie Aficionados; People Who Know Why Jerry Lewis Is So Popular In France. Let your list imagination run wild!

Here are the steps required to build your own Twitter list:

1. **Sign in to your Twitter account.**

2. **Click Home.**

3. **In your sidebar's Lists section, click New List.** Twitter displays the Create a New List dialog box.

4. **Type a list name and description.** By default, Twitter lists are available to all, but if you prefer your list to be a for-your-eyes-only affair, select the Private option.

5. **Click Create List.** Twitter displays your list and prompts you to add people to it.

To add someone to your list, you have a few options:

- If you know which user you want to add, go to the user's home page, click the Lists button, and then select the check box beside the list you want that user to be on. As you can see in Figure 4.21, Twitter adds your list to the user's home page.

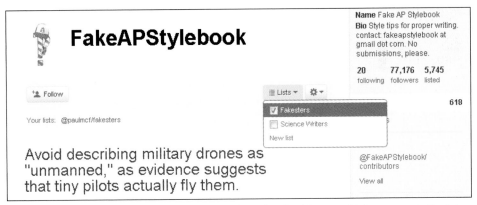

4.21 On a user's home page, click Lists and then select a list check box to add that person to the list.

- To add someone you follow, go to your home page, click Following, click the Lists button beside the user, and then select a list check box.

- To look for someone to add, click Find People and search for the person you want. In the search results, click the Lists button beside the user, and then select a list check box.

Working with Twitter Bots

Twitter is home to millions of people, but it's also a place where many nonhumans hang out. Yes, there are lots of companies and organizations on Twitter, but I'm talking here about a different kind of Twitter critter: the bot. A *bot* is an automated Twitter account that returns some kind of data in response to a specially formatted message. Some Twitter bots respond to reply messages, but most require direct messages, which means that you must follow the bot, and the bot then automatically follows you. (Remember that direct messaging requires mutual following. If you've protected your account, be sure to accept the bot's friend request when it comes in.)

In the rest of this chapter, I introduce you to Twitter's bot population by showing you how to interact with a few of the more useful bots.

Twitter bots are most useful when you've configured your account to send direct messages to you, either via e-mail (as described earlier in this chapter) or via your mobile phone (see Chapter 5).

Receiving a reminder message

Ask someone how he or she is doing these days, and more often than not you'll get an exasperated, "Busy!" as the response. We're all up to our eyeballs in meetings, chores, and other commitments, so it's not surprising that every now and then we forget one of those tasks, and all the apologizing we have to do puts us even further behind. Fortunately, you can use Twitter to avoid this fate. The Twitter bot named timer is an automated reminder service. You send it a direct message and a time, and when that time elapses timer sends you a direct message back.

To use timer, first go to http://twitter.com/timer and click the Follow button to follow this bot; it immediately follows you in return, so you're now set up to exchange direct messages with timer.

When you need a reminder, send a direct message to timer with the number of minutes after which you want the reminder sent (the minimum is 5 minutes), and the text you want timer to send back in the reminder message. For example, if you want to be reminded to call Karen in 30 minutes, your direct message will look like this:

```
30 Call Karen
```

If you're using the What's happening? text box to send the message, remember to include the d command and the timer username:

```
d timer 30 Call Karen
```

The timer bot is useful, but don't rely on it for accurate reminders. The timer bot seems to get around to sending the reminders when it's good and ready, so reminders are routinely a few minutes late.

Querying the Internet Movie Database

If you want to get some quick info on a movie or a movie personality, the famous Internet Movie Database (www.imdb.com) has a Twitter bot — named, not surprisingly, imdb — that's happy to serve. The imdb bot responds to either direct messages or reply messages.

To use direct messages, go to http://twitter.com/imdb and click the Follow button; the imdb bot follows you right back. Note, too, that the imdb account on Twitter also tweets regularly by sending out movie-related updates with themes such as Born On This Date, Trivia, and Quote.

If you don't want to receive the imdb tweets, bypass the following and send messages to @imdb instead.

If you want to get information about a movie, use the t command followed by the name of the movie:

```
d imdb t spinal tap
```

or

```
@imdb t spinal tap
```

If you know there are multiple versions of the movie, you can also specify the year:

```
d imdb t gladiator 2000
```

or

```
@imdb t gladiator 2000
```

To get information about a movie personality, use the p command followed by the person's name:

```
d imdb p clive owen
```

or

```
@imdb p clive owen
```

Getting a map

If you need a quick map of a city or town, use the Twitter 411 bot named t411. Go to http://twitter.com/t411 and click the Follow button; the t411 bot immediately follows you, too. You can now send your request using the following format:

```
d t411 map place
```

Here, *place* is the name of the city or town you want to see on a map. In response, you get a direct message with a URL. Click that address to see the map.

Translating text into another language

If you want to know how to say an English word or phrase in French, German, or some other language, or if you come across a foreign phrase that you want to convert to English, you can use the Twitter bot named twanslate. This is a direct message bot, so you first need to go to http://twitter.com/twanslate and click the Follow button. Once twanslate follows you back, you're good to go.

The first thing you should do is retrieve the twanslate help text by sending the following direct message:

```
d twanslate help
```

This text gives you the language abbreviations that you need to use in the twanslate commands. For example, the abbreviation for French is fr, so to translate the English phrase "I love Twitter" into French, you'd send the following message:

```
d twanslate fr I love Twitter
```

Getting a weather forecast

Want to know what the weather's going to be like where you are or where you're traveling to, but don't have access to a weather forecast? Now you do, thanks to the Twitter bot named forecast, which can provide a forecast for a given city or a given postal code.

The forecast bot uses direct messages, so first navigate to http://twitter.com/forecast and click the Follow button. Once the forecast bot returns the following favor, you can send your message. There are two ways to use the forecast bot: by city and by postal code.

To get the weather forecast for a city, send a direct message with the following format:

```
d forecast city, state
```

Replace *city* with the name of the city, and replace *state* with the two-letter state abbreviation. For example, the following direct message returns the forecast for Indianapolis, Indiana:

```
d forecast indianapolis, in
```

To get a weather forecast for a particular ZIP or postal code, send a direct message with the following format:

```
d forecast zip
```

Here, replace *zip* with the ZIP code of the location. For example, the following direct message returns the forecast for the 46256:

```
d forecast 46256
```

Returning Amazon data

Amazon.com stores a wealth of data about millions of books, DVDs, and albums, and now all of that data is at your fingertips, thanks to the Twitter bot named junglebot. This bot responds to direct messages, so first go to http://twitter.com/junglebot and click the Follow button. Once junglebot follows you back, you can use it to start querying Amazon.

You can use junglebot to return data about books, DVDs, or music using the following direct-message formats:

```
d junglebot book title
d junglebot dvd title
d junglebot music title
```

In each case, replace *title* with the name of the book, DVD, or music CD you want to work with. For example, to get information about the book *iPhone 3GS Portable Genius*, you'd send the following direct message:

```
d junglebot book iphone 3gs portable genius
```

Keeping up with the bots

The half-dozen bots that you learn about here really only scratch the surface of a burgeoning new Twitter field. New bots seem to come online every day, so how do you keep up? Perhaps the best way is the Twittter Fan Wiki, a wiki site that monitors all things Twitter, including bots. Check out the following page from time to time to see what's new in the Twitter bot landscape:

http://twitter.pbworks.com/Bots

Can I Use Twitter on My Mobile Phone?

1 2 3 4 5 6 7 8 9

The Twitter Web site is fine as far as sites go: It's simple to use and presents a nice, uncluttered interface. However, the fundamental element of the Twitter experience is *immediacy*: You think of or read or see something interesting, you send a tweet *now*; your friend posts an update, you read it *now*. Trying to do this on the Web isn't necessarily ideal because there are many hurdles between you and your tweets. If you want the true Twitter experience, your mobile phone is the way to go because you can post and read tweets right away, as you see in this chapter.

Understanding Twitter's Mobile Phone Feature

Twitter began life as a service for exchanging SMS (Short Message Service) messages, so mobile phones have been at the heart of the Twitter model from day one. As long as your phone is capable of working with text messages, and as long as your mobile provider rate plan includes a text-messaging component, you can send and receive tweets with your phone.

In the first part of this chapter I cover Twitter's built-in mobile phone commands and features. However, these days most people use third-party apps to interact with Twitter on their mobile phones, and that's probably the way you'll want to go yourself. I talk about Twitter phone apps later in this chapter.

Considering text message fees

Of course, it's one thing to have a text-messaging plan, but it's quite another not to go bankrupt with a text-messaging plan. How you use Twitter from your mobile phone (indeed, *whether* you use Twitter from your mobile phone) depends on the text-messaging rates set by your provider. There are three possibilities:

- **Your provider charges a per-message fee.** Many plans include a charge for each incoming and outgoing message (although some plans only charge one way, usually incoming). This might be as little as 10 cents a message, but it could be 15 or 20 cents a message.

- **Your provider sets a monthly message limit.** Some plans include a maximum number of messages per month (incoming or outgoing, but usually both) for a monthly fee. For example, you might get 300 messages for $5 a month. If you exceed that limit, a per-message charge applies.

- **Your provider gives you unlimited messages.** Almost all mobile providers offer unlimited plans for a monthly fee, typically around $20 a month.

Check with your provider to see what text-messaging plan you have, and consider adjusting the plan to match your expected Twitter usage. Obviously, if you're lucky enough to have unlimited text messaging, then you have no worries either sending or receiving Twitter updates on your phone. However, if you have to worry about per-message fees or monthly limits, then give this whole Twitter-on-your-mobile-phone thing some thought based on the tweeting patterns of you and your friends:

- **Sending tweets — you tweet only once in a while.** If you just post updates once or twice a day, then you won't run up exorbitant per-message charges or bump up against your monthly ceiling, so go ahead and Twitter away.

- **Sending tweets — you tweet frequently.** If you regularly post a dozen times a day or more, then you're either looking at monthly per-message fees totaling $30 or $40 or more, or you're looking at total monthly messages in the 300 to 400 range, or more. In this case, you probably want to consider the SMS alternatives I explain in the next section.

- **Receiving tweets.** Even if you only follow a few people, you're likely to receive hundreds of messages per month, and if you follow a few dozen people or more, then you're well into thousands of messages each month. For many tweeters, receiving updates on your mobile phone is only practical if you have an unlimited text-messaging plan.

Non-SMS Twitter alternatives

If you don't have text messaging on your mobile phone rate plan, or if you've done your calculations and it looks like your Twitter habit would put you in the poorhouse within months, does that mean the tweet-on-the-go world is out of reach? Not at all! You actually have several alternate routes to mobile Twittering:

- Use the version of Twitter's site designed for mobile Web browsers.

- Send your tweets via e-mail (yes, there's a trick to doing this).

- If your phone has a data plan and a Web browser, use one of the Web sites designed for mobile Twitter use, such as Hahlo.com.

- If you can add applications to your phone, install a Twitter mobile phone client such as TweetDeck or TwitterBerry.

You get to explore all of these techniques in this chapter.

Twitter's phone numbers

Once your phone is activated on Twitter (as described in the next section), you text updates and other commands to a special Twitter phone number. The number you use depends on where you live:

- **United States.** Use the short code number 40404.

- **Canada.** Use the short code number 21212.

- **Australia.** Use the short code number 0198089488 (Twitter currently supports only the provider Telstra).

- **Britain.** Use the short code number 86444 (Twitter currently supports the providers Vodafone, Orange, 3, and O2).

- **Haiti.** Use the short code 40404 (Twitter currently supports only the provider Digicel).

- **India.** Use the short code number 53000 (Twitter currently supports only the provider Bharti Airtel).

- **Indonesia.** Use the short code number 89887 (Twitter currently supports the providers AXIS and 3).

- **Ireland.** Use the short code number 51210 (Twitter currently supports only the provider O2).

- **New Zealand.** Use the short code number 8987 (Twitter currently supports the providers Vodafone and Telecom NZ).

- **Germany.** Use the long code number +49 17 6888 50505.

- **Sweden.** Use the long code number +46 737 494222.

- **Elsewhere.** Use the long code number +44 7624 801423.

Note that the short codes are two-way numbers (meaning you can send and receive messages), while the long codes are one-way numbers (meaning you can only send messages).

Twitter is quite strict with these numbers, meaning that, for example, if you live in the U.S., you must use the 40404 short code, and if you live somewhere other than the countries in the previous list, you must use the general international long code (+44 7624 801423). If you fall within the latter camp, be sure to check your rate plan very carefully for two things:

- Does your provider consider the number +44 7624 801423 to be an international call?

- If so, find out what it will charge you for each international message (it could be quite a lot).

note If you live in the U.S., Twitter allows you to send and receive unlimited messages using the 40404 short code. For everywhere else, you can only send and receive a total of 250 messages per week.

Activating Your Mobile Phone

Your first step toward using your phone with Twitter is to activate the phone in your Twitter account. Basically, you let Twitter know your phone number, and it then provides you with a code that you text to Twitter to confirm. Here are the specific steps:

1. **On your mobile phone, access the SMS feature, and then start a new message.**

2. **Use the phone's text-messaging interface to specify that you want the text sent to the Twitter phone number for your locale.**

3. **Type START and then send the message.** Twitter sends you back a message prompting you for your Twitter username (see Figure 5.1).

4. **Type your Twitter username and send the message.** Twitter sends you a message prompting you for your Twitter password (see Figure 5.2).

5. **Type your Twitter password and send the message.** Twitter sends you a message confirming that you can now use your phone with Twitter.

5.1 Text START and then, when prompted by Twitter, text your username to identify yourself.

5.2 To verify your mobile phone with Twitter HQ, you must text your account password.

To confirm that your phone is now on friendly terms with Twitter, sign in to your Twitter account, click Settings, and then click the Mobile tab. You should see your mobile phone number and the controls shown in Figure 5.3. I discuss these controls as you work through this chapter. For now, you're ready to starting sending updates through your phone!

Notice in Figure 5.3 that the Device updates setting is set to On by default. Don't be alarmed, however; that setting does *not* mean that you'll soon be inundated with your friend's tweets. Twitter turns off device updates for all the people you follow, so you won't see any incoming tweets until you turn on device updates for some friends. I cover this later in this chapter.

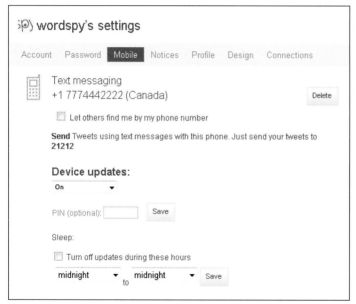

5.3 To make sure your mobile phone is verified, click Settings and then click the Mobile tab.

Sending an Update from Your Mobile Phone

Once your mobile phone is verified with Twitter, your phone becomes just another Twitter tool that you can use to post updates, send replies, fire off direct messages, and much more. The next few sections provide the details.

Sending an update from your mobile phone as text

The next time you're out and about without a computer in range and a perfectly tweetable thought, idea, or sight comes your way, pull out your trusty mobile phone and perform these almost-too-simple-to-be-true steps to post your update:

1. **On your mobile phone, access the SMS feature, and then start a new message.**

2. **Use the phone's text-messaging interface to specify that you want the text sent to the Twitter phone number for your locale.**

3. **Type your message.** Figure 5.4 shows an example.

4. **Send the message.** Your phone shoots the message to Twitter, and it then

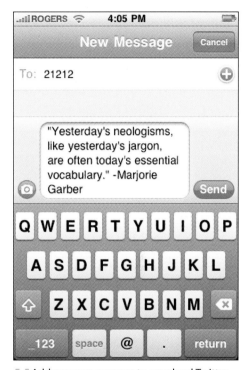

5.4 Address your message to your local Twitter phone number and then type your tweet text.

appears on your timeline, usually within a few seconds, as shown in Figure 5.5.

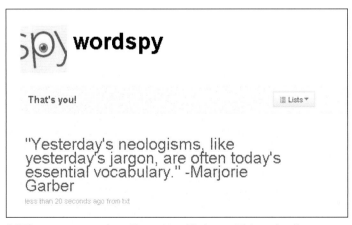

5.5 The text message from Figure 5.4 added to my Twitter timeline

Sending an update using Twitter's mobile Web site

There are lots of third-party tools you can use to manage your Twitter account using your mobile phone, and you learn about many of them later in this chapter. And you've seen that you can also use your phone's SMS feature to send tweets. However, what if you don't want to install a Twitter application on your phone, or if your phone doesn't support third-party programs? Or what if your mobile phone plan doesn't include text messaging, or it charges big-time fees for each message?

If your phone includes a mobile Web browser and you have a data plan, then you can work around each of these problems by using Twitter's mobile Web site to send your tweets. This site is optimized for the small screens that are typical of mobile phones, so you can tweet to your heart's content while you're on the go.

Here are the steps to follow:

1. **Point your mobile Web browser to http://mobile.twitter.com/.** Twitter redirects the browser to the mobile Twitter page.

2. **Select Sign In.** Twitter takes you to the login page.

3. **Use the Username or Email text box to enter your Twitter username.**

4. **Use the Password text box to enter your Twitter password.**

5. **Select Sign In.** Twitter takes you to your home page, which appears something like the screen shown in Figure 5.6.

6. **Type your update text in the What's happening? box.**

7. **Choose Tweet.** Twitter sends your update.

5.6 You can use Twitter's mobile Web site to post an update from your mobile phone or PDA.

8. **Scroll down to the bottom of the page and click Sign Out.** Twitter logs you out of your account.

note If you tried Twitter's original mobile site (http://m.twitter.com/) a while back, were disappointed, and decided never to go back, it may be time to pay a return visit. The new site (http://mobile.twitter.com/) is much more functional. For example, you can now see not just your friend timeline, but also your mentions, favorites, and direct messages. You can also reply to and retweet updates, mark a tweet as a favorite, search Twitter, and more.

Sending an update from your mobile phone as e-mail

If you don't want to tweet via SMS (because you don't have a text-messaging plan or the plan you have is not Twitter friendly) and you can't use the Twitter mobile site (say, because you don't have a data plan), it's still possible to post updates by phone (although not to receive updates). The trick here is a bit convoluted, but it works. What you're going to do is take advantage of two features that are available from various services on the Web:

- **E-mail-to-blog.** This is a feature that provides you with a special e-mail address, and any messages you send to that address are automatically posted to your blog. Blog hosts such as Blogger, TypePad, and WordPress support this feature.

- **Blog feed-to-Twitter.** This is a feature that monitors your blog's RSS feed and automatically sends new posts to your Twitter account. Services such as Twitterfeed and SocialOomph offer this feature.

In other words, your tweet-by-e-mail process works like this:

1. **Use your mobile phone to send an e-mail message to your blog's e-mail address.**
2. **Your blog host posts that message to your blog.**
3. **Your Twitter application detects the new post via your blog's RSS feed.**
4. **Your Twitter application sends the post text as an update to your Twitter account.**

Like I said, it's a bit of a circuitous route, but it doesn't take all that long to set up, and once it's running you never have to give it a second thought.

So your first chore is to set up and configure a blog on a host that offers the e-mail-to-blog feature. Here are some options:

- **Blogger.** Go to www.blogger.com and create a new blog (it's free). Click the Settings tab, click Email & Mobile, add text to the Email Posting Address text box to complete your posting address, and then click Save Settings.

- **TypePad.** Go to www.typepad.com and create a new blog (plans start at $8.95 a month). Click your blog, click the Settings tab, click Post by Email, and then make a note of the Secret Address.

- **WordPress.** You need to be using the full version of WordPress available from http://wordpress.org (the hosted version at http://wordpress.com doesn't offer the Post via E-mail feature) or sign up for a WordPress blog host. See the instructions at http://codex.wordpress.org/Blog_by_Email.

- **LiveJournal.** Go to www.livejournal.com and create a free blog. Click the Manage Account link, and then click the Mobile tab. In the Email Posting section, fill in an address and a PIN, and then click Save.

- **Windows Live Spaces.** Create a free blog at http://spaces.live.com. In your space, choose Options ⇨ More options, and then click E-mail publishing. Select the Turn on e-mail publishing check box, fill in the fields, and then click Save.

Be sure to guard the e-mail address you use for posting to your blog. Otherwise, anyone who knows the address can post to your blog, and therefore also to your Twitter account!

The tweet uses the format *Subject*: *Body*, where *Subject* is the e-mail message subject line and *Body* is the e-mail text.

With your blog host's e-mail-to-blog feature set up, the next step is to get your blog's feed into Twitter. Here are two services to check out:

- **Twitterfeed (http://twitterfeed.com).** This site forwards blog feeds to Twitter and other sites. See Chapter 9 to learn how to add your blog feed to this site.

- **SocialOomph (http://socialoomph.com).** This site offers a smorgasbord of Twitter features. The free version doesn't offer an RSS-to-Twitter feature, but the Professional version does (although it costs about $30 per month, so it's a bit steep just for this).

Now you're good to go. Use your mobile phone to fire off an e-mail message to your blog host's e-mail-to-blog address, as shown in Figure 5.7.

After a while (it depends on how frequently you set up Twitterfeed to check for fresh posts), your message shows up as a tweet on your Twitter account, as shown in Figure 5.8.

5.7 Use your phone's e-mail application to send the tweet text to your blog host's e-mail-to-blog address.

If you use Twitterfeed, be sure to deselect the Post Link check box in the Advanced Settings section. Otherwise, your tweet includes a link to your blog "post," which is not what you want.

paulmcf

That's you!   ☰ Lists ▾

Hunh?: The dude who wrote a book
called "Nerds" now thinks the word
"nerd" should be banned! http://is.gd
/5xK5i

half a minute ago from twitterfeed

5.8 The email message is eventually forwarded as an update on your Twitter account.

Sending a reply from your mobile phone

Replies are open to anyone whose account isn't protected, so you can reply to *any* Twitter user from your phone. This is great if you want to send a witty retort while you're out and about. Here's how it's done:

1. **On your mobile phone, access the SMS feature and start a new message.**

2. **Enter the Twitter phone number for your locale.**

3. **Type @ followed by the Twitter username of the person you want to reply to.** Be sure to add at least one space after the username.

4. **Type the rest of your message.** Figure 5.9 shows an example reply.

5.9 To reply, send a message that begins with @ *username* to your local Twitter phone number.

5. **Send the message.** Your phone hands the message off to Twitter, and it then appears on your timeline, usually within a few seconds, as shown in Figure 5.10.

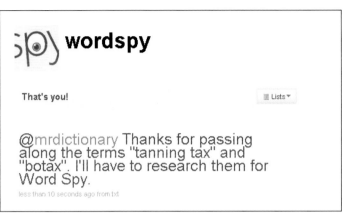

5.10 The reply message from Figure 5.9 added to my Twitter timeline

Sending a direct message from your mobile phone

If you're in a mutual-follow Twitter connection with someone, you can drop that person a direct message. If you happen to be running around town or stuck in a meeting and you think of something you want to tell your friend directly, you can post the direct message right from your mobile phone. Here are the steps to follow:

1. **On your mobile phone, access the SMS feature, and then start a new message.**

2. **Type the Twitter phone number for your locale.**

3. **Type d followed by the Twitter username of the person you want to direct-message.** Be sure to add at least one space after the username.

4. **Type the rest of your message.**

5. **Send the message.** Your phone sends the message, and before too long it appears in that person's Direct Messages timeline.

Protecting your updates with a PIN number

The malicious hackers of the world are, to be charitable, a resourceful bunch, and it seems there's no service in the world they haven't cracked. That includes SMS, where there are now tools available online that enable evildoers to spoof SMS messages as long as they know the mobile number of the person being duped.

To guard against such attacks, Twitter offers a security feature called a PIN (personal identification number), which is a four-digit number that (ideally) only you know. When you add a PIN to your Twitter account, you can only post an update from your mobile phone if that text message begins with your four-digit PIN. No PIN, no post.

If you're concerned about SMS spoofing (and while it's not a huge deal right now, it could easily become a problem one of these days), follow these steps to protect your mobile updates:

1. **Sign in to your Twitter account.**
2. **Click Settings.** Your account settings appear.
3. **Click the Mobile tab.**
4. **Type a four-digit number in the PIN text box, as shown in Figure 5.11.**
5. **Click Save.** Twitter saves the new setting, and you must now precede all mobile phone messages with your PIN.

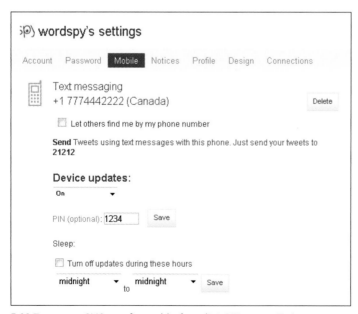

5.11 To prevent SMS spoofing, add a four-digit PIN to your Twitter account.

Following Twitterers on Your Mobile Phone

Although most Twitterers use their mobile phones to send tweets, replies, and direct messages, you can also use mobile text messages to handle various following and friend chores: follow new people, stop following people, receive a friend's updates and direct messages, get a person's Twitter profile, and much more. The next few sections take you through the details.

Following a person from your mobile phone

So you're at a cocktail party and you mention that your favorite writer is Steven Johnson (author of *Everything Bad Is Good for You*, among others), and someone tells you that he has a Twitter account and this person even knows his username: stevenbjohnson. That's not hard to remember, but you know that if you don't do something right away, you'll forget to follow your literary hero. Fortunately, you can pull out your trusty mobile phone and immediately update your Twitter account to follow him. Nice! Here's how it's done:

1. **Open your mobile phone's SMS feature and start a new message.**

2. **Type the Twitter phone number for your location.**

3. **Type FOLLOW.**

> **note** Twitter's text commands aren't case sensitive, so it doesn't matter if you use FOLLOW or follow (or even FoLlOw, for that matter).

4. **Type a space and then the Twitter username of the person you want to follow.**

5. **Send the message.** When Twitter receives the command, it updates your friend list to include the user and then sends you back a confirmation message, as shown in Figure 5.12.

5.12 To follow a user, send a text with a follow *username*, and then Twitter sends you a confirmation message.

note Although you can stop receiving a person's tweets on your mobile phone (as shown in Figure 5.12), it's not possible to stop following a person from your mobile phone. To stop following someone, you have to use the Twitter Web site.

Receiving a person's tweets on your mobile phone

When you first activate your mobile phone with Twitter, it turns on the device notifications setting, which means that you've authorized Twitter to send you stuff. At first, this just means you receive the following:

- **Results of commands you've sent.** For example, if you send follow *username* to start following someone, Twitter sends you a message in return to acknowledge that you're now following that person (as you saw earlier in Figure 5.12).

- **Direct messages sent to you.** These could be direct messages sent from people you follow (and who follow you) or the results of a command you sent to a Twitter bot.

If you also want to get the tweets posted by someone you follow delivered to your mobile phone, then you must activate mobile device updates for that person. Twitter gives you various ways to do this, depending on where you are in the Twitter interface:

- **In the list of people you follow.** Each user has a mobile phone icon that appears gray when you're not getting that person's tweets sent to your phone, and green when you are getting the updates (see Figure 5.13). The default setting is to not receive tweets, unless you followed that person using a mobile phone message, in which case the default setting is to receive the user's tweets. If the icon is currently off (gray), click it to toggle the setting on (green).

- **On a person's profile page.** You see the same mobile phone icon, so if the icon is currently off (gray), click it to toggle the setting on (green).

- **On your mobile phone.** Text the command ON *username*, where *username* is the Twitter screen name of the person whose tweets you want on your phone.

You follow 21 people add or invite more

User / Name

stevenbjohnson ✓
Steven Johnson
A Victorian winter wonderland on our block in Park
Slope http://twitpic.com/u9ltm 8:18 PM Dec 19th

Updates are sent by SMS to your mobile phone.

Actions

Fritinancy
Nancy Friedman | Oakland, CA
RT @ellentparker: RT @thefastertimes Best American
Short Stories in Titles http://bit.ly/5xBxeN (most-used
word? "Life") about 7 hours ago

CityDictionary
City Dictionary | Madison, WI
Word of the Day - Trustafarian: Boulder, CO
http://www.citydictionary.com
#wotd about 16 hours ago

5.13 To receive a person's updates on your mobile phone, toggle the mobile phone icon to the green state.

There may be a user for whom you don't want to see every tweet on your phone, just the occasional one. In that case, configure your account to not receive that person's tweets. To retrieve the latest tweet from that person, use your phone to text the command GET *username*, where *username* is the person's Twitter screen name.

Marking an update as a favorite from your mobile phone

Once you start getting updates on your mobile phone, you never know when a particularly good tweet might come your way. In fact, you might receive a tweet that's so good you want to add it to

your Favorites timeline. How can you do that without a Web browser? Use your phone, of course! Here's how:

1. **Start your phone's SMS tool and launch a new message.**

2. **Type your location's Twitter phone number.**

3. **Type FAV.**

4. **Type a space and then the Twitter username of the person whose tweet you want to favorite.**

5. **Send the message.** Twitter adds the user's most recent message to your Favorites timeline and sends you back a confirmation message.

Twitter favorites the most recent tweet by the user, so if you're dealing with a prolific tweeter, be sure to text the FAV command as soon as possible.

Retrieving a profile on your mobile phone

When you're on the Twitter Web site you can view a person's profile page to find out a bit about him or her: name, location, Web site, and one-line bio. If you need the same information while away from Twitter, you can use your mobile phone to retrieve it. Follow these steps:

1. **Open the SMS application on your phone and start a new message.**

2. **Type your Twitter phone number.**

3. **Type WHOIS.**

4. **Type a space and then the username of the person you're curious about.**

5. **Send the message.** Twitter returns a text message with the user's profile information, as shown in Figure 5.14.

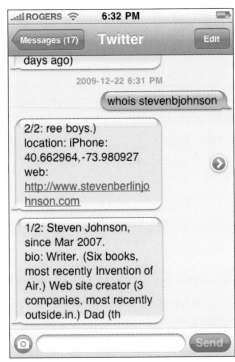

5.14 Text WHOIS *username* to receive the profile information of a Twitter user.

Stopping a person's updates on your mobile phone

If you're receiving a person's tweets on your mobile phone, you may find that the updates aren't as good as you thought or can wait until the next time you're online. Similarly, you might have turned on Device updates for a few too many friends, and now your mobile phone's SMS inbox is stuffed. Either way, you might want to stop a person's update from going to your phone, and once again Twitter gives you multiple methods. The one you choose depends on where you're located in the Twitterverse:

- **In the list of people you follow.** Locate the user's mobile phone icon. If the icon is currently on (green), click it to toggle the setting off (gray).

- **On a person's profile page.** Locate the user's mobile phone icon. If the icon is currently on (green), click it to toggle the setting off (gray).

- **On your mobile phone.** Text the command OFF *username*, where *username* is the Twitter screen name of the person whose updates you no longer require.

Receiving only direct messages on your mobile phone

For many tweeters, their friend timeline is something they watch with varying degrees of interest, particularly if they follow dozens or hundreds of people. For these users, the real meat of their Twitter experience lies in the direct messages they receive from mutual friends. If you fall into this camp, then you might want to configure your account device settings to send only direct messages to your mobile phone. Here's how:

1. **Sign in to your Twitter account.**
2. **Click Settings.** Your account settings appear.
3. **Click the Mobile tab.**
4. **Use the Device updates list to choose Direct Messages, as shown in Figure 5.15.**
5. **Click Save.** Twitter saves the new setting, and now only sends direct messages to your mobile phone.

wordspy's settings

Account   Password   **Mobile**   Notices   Profile   Design   Connections

Text messaging
+1 7774442222 (Canada)   Delete

☐ Let others find me by my phone number

Send Tweets using text messages with this phone. Just send your tweets to
21212

Device updates:

On   ▼
On
Off
Direct Messages   Save

Sleep:

☐ Turn off updates during these hours

midnight   ▼   midnight   ▼   Save
              to

5.15 In the Device updates list, choose Direct Messages to have only direct
messages sent to your phone.

Stopping all updates on your mobile phone

If you've activated Device updates for a number of your friends, you might start feeling a bit
overwhelmed if they start tossing dozens of tweets a day at your phone. If you want to take a
break and catch up, don't go through the hassle of turning off Device updates for every person.
Instead, you can tell Twitter to stop sending you any updates. You can do this either on the Twitter
site or using your phone.

Follow these steps to turn off Device updates using the Twitter Web site:

1. **Sign in to your Twitter account.**

2. **Click Settings.** Your account settings appear.

3. **Click the Mobile tab.**

4. **Use the Device updates list to choose Off.**

5. **Click Save.** Twitter saves the new setting and no longer sends any Device updates to
   your mobile phone.

When you're ready to resume updates (and direct messages, if you turned those off, too), open your settings on the Twitter site and choose On in the Device updates list or, from your mobile phone, text the command ON to your local Twitter number.

Here are the steps to follow to turn off Device updates from your mobile phone:

1. **Start the SMS tool on your phone and begin a new message.**
2. **Type the Twitter phone number for your locale.**
3. **Type OFF.**
4. **Send the message.** Twitter turns off Device updates and sends you a confirmation message.

If you also want to prevent Twitter from sending direct messages to your mobile phone, wait until you get the response from Twitter for the OFF command, and then text a second OFF command to your local Twitter number.

Sending a Twitter invitation from your mobile phone

Although it's still loads of fun to follow complete strangers on Twitter (assuming, of course, that those strangers have the mental wherewithal to be interesting or at least fun), Twitter's appeal grows exponentially with each new real-world friend you can follow. If you know of someone who's not currently on Twitter, but you'd like her to be, then you can use your mobile phone to extend a Twitter invitation to that person's mobile phone. Give it a whirl:

1. **Fire up your mobile phone's SMS application and start a new message.**
2. **Type your Twitter phone number.**
3. **Type INVITE.**
4. **Type a space and then the mobile phone number of the person you're inviting.**
5. **Send the message.** Twitter sends an invitation SMS message to your friend's mobile phone. The message looks like this (where *yourname* is your Twitter username):

```
yourname invited you to Twitter! Reply with your
name to start. Standard message charges apply, send
'stop' to quit. help@twitter.com for help.
```

Getting your Twitter stats on your mobile phone

Want a quick update on the number of people who are following you and the number of people you're following? Easier done than said because you can get that data sent right to your phone. Here's how:

1. **Use your mobile phone's SMS application to begin a new message.**

2. **Type your Twitter phone number.**

3. **Type STATS.**

4. **Send the message.** Twitter texts you back a message with your follower and following numbers.

A Summary of Twitter's Text Commands

I've gone through quite a few text commands in this chapter, so now's a good time to pause and take in the bird's-eye view of things. Table 5.1 presents a list of all the text commands you can use from your mobile phone.

Table 5.1 Twitter's Text Commands

Command	What It Does
message	Posts *message* as a tweet.
@*username message*	Sends a reply to *username*.
D *username message*	Sends a direct message to *username*.
FOLLOW *username*	Configures your Twitter profile to follow *username*.
FAV *username*	Marks *username*'s most recent tweet as a favorite.
WHOIS *username*	Returns the profile information for *username*.
ON *username*	Turns on Device updates for *username*.
OFF *username*	Turns off Device updates for *username*. (You can also use the LEAVE command.)
GET *username*	Returns the most recent tweet posted by *username*.
OFF	Turns off Device updates for all users. Send OFF again to also turn off direct messages.
ON	Turns on Device updates and direct messages.
STOP	Stops Twitter from sending all messages to your phone immediately. (You can also use the QUIT command.)
INVITE *phone number*	Sends an SMS invitation to a friend's mobile *phone number*.
STATS	Returns your number of followers, how many people you're following, and which words you're tracking.

You can also use the commands in Table 5.1 in the Twitter Web site (for example, in the What's happening? text box) as well as in most Twitter clients.

Tools for Managing Twitter from Your Mobile Phone

Once you've done the Twitter thing on your mobile phone for a while, you realize that it has its pros and cons:

- On the pro side, it's fantastic to be able to post, reply, and send direct messages wherever you happen to be, to follow folks right away, and to see updates in real time.

- On the con side, the command-line style interface leaves something to be desired. The Twitter Web site is nice because it comes with little icons and controls that you can simply click to send replies, favorite a tweet, view a user's profile, and more.

Wouldn't it be great if you could somehow combine the immediacy of a mobile phone with the convenience of the Twitter site? Yes, it certainly would. Happily, other people with more programming skills than you or I have thought of this, too, and they've gone and done something about it. A couple of things, actually:

- **Applications.** There are now lots of Twitter client applications available that you can install on your mobile phone (if your phone supports that kind of thing).

- **Web sites.** There are also a number of Twitter-focused Web sites available that are optimized for mobile phones (if your phone has a mobile Web browser and you've got a data plan from your provider).

In both cases, you get immediacy because you're managing your Twitter account from a mobile device, but you also get convenience because the applications and sites offer snazzy interfaces that make it easy to perform most common Twitter tasks. The rest of this chapter takes you through a few of these tools so you can get an idea what's out there.

The collection of applications and Web sites that I list here isn't even remotely comprehensive. If you want more, the best place to go is the Mobile Apps page of the Twitter Fan Wiki: http://twitter.pbworks.com/Mobile-Apps.

Mobile phone applications for Twitter

If your mobile phone supports third-party applications, then installing a Twitter client program is a great way to go because the program works anywhere you have a data connection, whether it's on the cellular network or via a network connection such as Wi-Fi or Bluetooth. The next few sections take quick looks at a few interesting Twitter programs.

I'm assuming here that you know how to install applications on your mobile phone. See your manual if all this is new to you.

Twitter for iPhone

If you use an iPhone (or an iPod touch), give the official Twitter client (formerly known as Tweetie) a test drive (it's free!). Once it's downloaded and installed, tap the new Twitter icon. The program displays the Add Account screen initially, so enter your Twitter username and password, tap Done, and then tap your account. Twitter immediately downloads your friend timeline, as shown in Figure 5.16. Use the icons along the bottom of the screen to surf your other timelines: Mentions, Direct Messages, Search, and Lists.

Tap a tweet to open it. As you can see in Figure 5.17, you get several tweet-related icons at the bottom: Reply, Link (e-mail or repost the tweet's link), and Favorite. Tap the Actions icon (it's the one on the right) to get a long menu of commands, including Retweet and Quote Tweet.

5.16 A friend timeline displayed in the Twitter for iPhone app

TweetDeck

If you're more of a Twitter power user with an iPhone (or iPod touch), consider loading TweetDeck onto your iPhone. This powerful application does just about everything a Twitter client should (and more!), and all with a nice interface to boot. (Even better, it's available *free* from the App Store.) After you start the program and enter your

Twitter account credentials, tap All Friends, and TweetDeck displays your friend timeline, as shown in Figure 5.18.

Tap the Columns icon in the toolbar at the bottom of the screen to switch from one section of the program to another: Mentions, DM (direct messages), Favorites, and so on. Flick the screen right and left to see the columns, and then tap the one you want to work with. You can also tap Add Column to display more columns for things like custom Twitter searches. (If you also use the desktop version of TweetDeck, which I talk about in Chapter 8, you can sign up for an account on Twitter's servers and sync your columns between the app and the desktop program.) There's plenty here to keep you busy for a long time.

To work with a tweet, tap it and you then see a screen that looks like the one shown in Figure 5.19. This is a power user's dream, with icons for replying, sending a direct message, retweeting, e-mailing, and favoriting the tweet. You can also tap the user to see that person's profile.

5.17 Tap a tweet and the tweet commands appear as icons at the bottom of the screen.

5.18 The friend timeline in TweetDeck

TweetDeck also supports multiple Twitter accounts, which is a gotta-have-it feature if, like me, you manage multiple Twitter identities.

Twitter for BlackBerry

Twitter for BlackBerry is the official BlackBerry Twitter app that was developed jointly by the Twitter team and Research in Motion (the makers of the BlackBerry). It's an excellent Twitter client that runs on most BlackBerry devices, including the Storm, Bold, Curve, and Pearl. Twitter for BlackBerry is free, and you can download it either from the BlackBerry App Store or from blackberry.com/twitter.

When you first start Twitter for BlackBerry, the program asks for your Twitter account credentials. Enter your Twitter username and password and then select Login to display the Home screen. The Home screen offers the classic What's happening? prompt, as shown in Figure 5.20. You enter your update message in the text box (a characters available line counts down to 0), then you select Update to post your tweet.

5.20 You use Twitter for BlackBerry Home screen to post tweets.

5.19 Tap and hold a tweet to see a satisfyingly large number of tweet options.

You use the icons at the top of the screen to switch from one Twitter for BlackBerry screen to another. Here are the icons from left to right:

- **Home.** This screen shows not only the What's happening? text box, but also a list of the tweets posted by the people you follow (see Figure 5.21).

- **Mentions.** Displays the replies people have sent you as well as your other mentions.

- **My Lists.** Displays your Twitter lists.

- **My Profile.** Displays your Twitter profile data.

- **Direct Messages.** Displays the direct messages people have sent you.

- **Find People.** Lets you search for tweeters.

- **Search.** Lets you search for tweets.

- **Popular Topics.** Displays a list of topics that are currently trending on Twitter.

5.21 Twitter for BlackBerry's Home screen also displays the tweets posted by the folks you follow.

To work with a tweet, select it and then use the options menu to select a command, such as Reply, Favorite, or Retweet.

TinyTwitter

TinyTwitter is a neat little program that packs a lot of features into its tiny frame. It has a Java version that should work on any BlackBerry as well as any phone that supports Java applications, and a separate version that works on Windows Mobile-based PocketPCs and Smartphones. Navigate to www.tinytwitter.com to download it for free.

When you first start the program you're prompted for your Twitter credentials. Enter your username and password, and then choose Done from the menu to sign in to your Twitter account. By default, TinyTwitter displays your friend timeline, as shown in Figure 5.22. Select a tweet to read it.

TinyTwitter's menu is crammed with useful commands:

- **Update.** Refreshes the current timeline.

- **Tweet.** Displays a text box so you can send an update.

- **Access Links.** Displays the links that appear in the highlighted tweet.

- **Reply.** Sends a reply to the person who sent the highlighted tweet.

- **Reply All.** Sends a reply to the person who sent the highlighted tweet, as well as every other Twitter username included in the tweet.

- **Direct.** Sends a direct message to the person who sent the highlighted tweet.

- **Favorite.** Marks the highlighted tweet as a favorite.

- **Retweets.** Retweets the highlighted tweet.

- **User Timeline.** Returns the list of tweets posted by the person who sent the highlighted tweet.

- **Unfollow.** Stops following the highlighted user.

- **Delete.** Deletes the highlighted tweet.

- **Delete All.** Deletes all the tweets.

- **Inbox.** Displays the replies and direct messages people have sent you.

- **Nearby Twitter Peeps.** Looks for users who are near your location (if your phone supports GPS).

- **Search.** Lets you search Twitter.

NS newscientist: Since we blogged about DeCode Genetics, the firm has removed the assessment of Alzheimer's risk from its analysis http://bit.ly/6vQAfk
7m 16s ago bit.ly

NS newscientist: The shape of gifts to

grahamfarmelo: Two of this year's

NS newscientist: Move over,

TweetDeck: I just voted for TweetDeck

NS newscientist: 50 years of waiting for

grahamfarmelo: Maureen Dowd

BadAstronomer: You don't normally

TUAW: Blackberry issues? It's not just

DanielPink: RT @TEDchris: Here it is!

johnemcintyre: Some days I'm less

BadAstronomer: Or really funny. One

BadAstronomer: Just recorded w/

5.22 TinyTwitter shows your friend timeline initially.

- **What's Hot.** Displays the latest Twitter trends.

- **Public Timeline.** Shows Twitter's public timeline (tweets from all unprotected accounts).

- **Hide Friends.** Enables you to hide the tweets from selected friends.

- **Credentials.** Enables you to change your Twitter account username and password.

More mobile phone applications

The perfect mobile Twitter application is a kind of Holy Grail for gadget-obsessed tweeters, one that they seek constantly but fear they'll never find. If you're on the same quest, here are a few other applications to consider:

- **Blackbird.** This is a basic Twitter client for BlackBerry mobile phones. See http://dossy.org/twitter/blackbird/.

- **ceTwit.** This is a full-featured Windows Mobile 6 client, available from www.kosertech.com/blog/?page_id=5.

- **HootSuite.** This is an iPhone (or iPod Touch) application that you can download from the App Store for $1.99. This is a major-league app that's bursting at the seams with features, including multiple-account support, Twitter lists, and scheduling tweets for future delivery.

- **OpenBeak.** This is a nice Twitter client (it used to be called TwitterBerry) that runs on most BlackBerry devices, including Storm, Bold, Curve, and Pearl. OpenBeak is free, and you can download it from www.orangetame.com/products/openbeak/.

- **Pocketwit.** This is a nice Windows Mobile 6 (or later) application with an interesting interface. See http://code.google.com/p/pocketwit/.

- **Twitterrific.** If your needs are simple, give this iPhone (or iPod touch) client a test drive. The App Store offers a free version that displays ads within your timelines, as well as Twitterific Premium, an ad-free version that costs $4.99.

- **Twidroid.** This is a full-featured application designed for Android mobile phones. See http://twidroid.com.

- **Twittelator Pro.** This is an iPhone (or iPod Touch) application that you can download from the App Store for $4.99. This is a full-featured app that also supports multiple Twitter accounts.

- **TwitToday.** This is a free Windows Mobile 5 (or later) widget that installs a Twitter text box on your Today screen, so you can quickly send a tweet. It's available from http://dalelane.co.uk/page.php?id=1047.

- **Twobile.** This is a Windows Mobile 5 (or later) application that is free, but surprisingly full featured. As I write this, Twobile only supports touch-screen phones. You can get it here: www.infinitumsoftware.com/twobile.

- **UberTwitter.** This is a simple, functional, and free Twitter client designed for the BlackBerry. Get it here: www.ubertwitter.com/.

Mobile phone Web sites for Twitter

If your mobile phone doesn't support third-party applications, or you just don't want to load outside applications on your phone, you can still get full-featured Twitter goodness by heading out to the Web with your phone's mobile browser. Web sites optimized for mobile phone Twittering aren't as powerful as the best mobile applications, and they're slower by a long shot, but they're still way more friendly than SMS, and they're all more powerful and feature filled than the Twitter mobile site at http://mobile.twitter.com.

Dabr

The Dabr site (http://dabr.co.uk/) takes the official Twitter mobile site idea and runs with it. That is, it takes the simple interface of mobile.twitter.com and bolts on useful tweeter-friendly features such as your friend timeline, lists of the replies and directs you've received, Twitter search, lists of your favorites, followers, and friends, the public Twitter timeline, and more.

5.23 The Dabr main page shows your friend timeline and an update text box.

Once you sign in to your account, you see the Dabr main page, which not only offers a tweet text box, just like mobile.twitter.com, but also your friend timeline, as shown in Figure 5.23. This is a sensible setup because you get the two most important Twitter features right up front. You use the toolbar across the top of the page to switch features.

Hahlo

The Hahlo Web site (http://hahlo.com/) works best with the iPhone. The home page offers text boxes for your Twitter username and password, and once you're signed in you see Hahlo's version of your friend timeline, as shown in Figure 5.24. For each tweet, you get clickable links, plus when you tap a tweet you see icons that enable you to reply, retweet, or favorite the update, as well as send a direct message to the tweeter.

To configure Hahlo to load a different page at startup, tap Menu, and then tap Settings. Tap the Custom Home list, tap the page you'd prefer to load initially, tap Done, and then tap Save Settings.

5.24 By default, you see your friend timeline when you log in to the Hahlo mobile Web site.

Tap the Messages tab to see your update timeline, and tap the Mentions tab to see the tweets that include your username.

When you're ready to send an update, tap the TWEET icon in the upper-right corner of the screen. Hahlo presents you with a standard text box and displays the number of characters you have left as you type (see Figure 5.25).

Twitter power users will want to dive in to the many other features available on Hahlo, all of which you can see by tapping the MENU icon at the top of the screen. Hahlo pops up a window that contains a dozen icons that represent all of Hahlo's features, plus a sophisticated Search tool, as you can see in Figure 5.26.

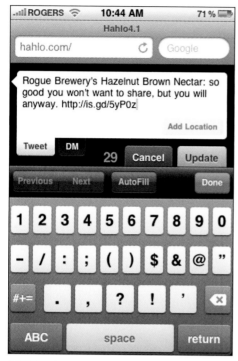

5.25 Tapping out a tweet using the Hahlo mobile Web site

5.26 Tap MENU to see this surprisingly long list of all Hahlo's other Twitter features.

More mobile phone sites for Twitter

To round out this look at Twitter Web sites that are mobile friendly, here's a list of a few more sites that you can try:

- **Mobile Tweete.** http://m.tweete.net/
- **Slandr.** http://m.slandr.net/
- **Twitter2Go.** http://twitter2go.com

How Do I Find Stuff in Twitter?

1 2 3 4 5 **6** 7 8 9

Twitter users are clearly a talkative bunch, sending out nearly 50 million tweets every day, according to stats provided by Twitter HQ (a number that will surely grow over time). The total number of tweets posted hit 10 billion in the spring of 2010, a stat that at first blush seems intimidating, but with a bit of thought turns into an opportunity. After all, 10 billion tweets represent a lot of information, much of it actually useful, so Twitter's database must be a gold mine of knowledge on almost any subject. But how do you extract that gold? By taking advantage of Twitter's useful search engine, as well as the eyebrow-raisingly large collection of third-party Twitter search tools, as you see in this chapter.

Running a Basic Search

If you have a word or phrase that interests you and you want to see if your fellow Twitter users have been interested enough in the same term to tweet about it, the Twitter search engine can let you know. You can use it to search Twitter for a word, multiple words, or an exact phrase. Twitter takes your search text and looks for tweets that include matches in the tweet text or in the username of the tweeter.

Here are the steps to follow to run a basic Twitter search:

1. **Log in to your Twitter account.**

2. **Click Home.**

3. **Type your search term into the Search text box, as shown in Figure 6.1.**

4. **Press Enter or Return.** You can also click the Search Twitter icon (the magnifying glass) to the right of the search box.

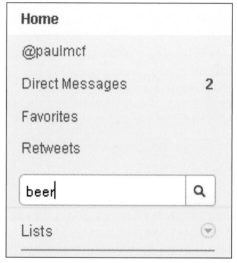

6.1 To begin a Twitter search, type a search term in the Search text box and then press Enter.

Twitter then replaces your home page timeline with the search results, as shown in Figure 6.2. The main part of the page shows the heading Real-time results for *term,* where *term* is the search word you typed. Below that you see a list of tweets that include your search term, ordered chronologically with the most recently posted tweet at the top.

 One of the nice features of the Twitter search interface is that you can save searches for later use. If you have a frequently used search query, run the search and then click Save this search that appears at the top of the results. Twitter adds a link below the Search box and you can run the search any time by just clicking that link.

Real-time results for beer   ⊕ Save this search

oskarblues **Beer** Soaked Blog Update: Happy Holiday's & NYE
Packages #oskarblues
half a minute ago from Twitter Tools

debbierosenbaum Vaca summary: uber hot, first scubadive,
colombian familia, **beer** in the streets, frozen lemonades in the pool
at sunset. Pics soon. Awesome.
half a minute ago from TwitterBerry

hiro_t_hiro_t @Naglfer **Beer**!Neer!なら仕方ないですなwww
less than a minute ago from Tween

kevthulhu Just cracked my first imaginary **beer** of the day.
less than a minute ago from Digsby

andymboyle @grantmeaccess I drank with Matt! I almost threw a
beer st him because he doesn't consider Nebraska the Midwest.
Nice guy.
less than a minute ago from Tweetie

6.2 The Twitter search results appear on your Twitter home page and
matching tweets appear in chronological order.

Real-time search results

Whatever type of search you perform, you see the matching tweets under the heading Real-time
results for *term*, where *term* is the search text you typed. The use of the word *real-time* means not
only that you're seeing the most recently posted tweets that match your search term, but that
Twitter is tracking your search term in the background while your results are displayed. If any new
tweets are posted while you're checking out the results, Twitter adds a banner above the results:

```
x more results since you started searching.
```

Here, *x* is the number of new results. You probably won't see this banner for obscure search terms,
but if your search is related to some topic that currently has lots of Twitter buzz, the banner might
appear surprisingly quickly. For example, I ran a search on "beer," obviously a popular (and,
admittedly, overly general) term, and within a few seconds Twitter displayed the banner shown in
Figure 6.3 to tell me that 12 new matching tweets had been posted.

6.3 If any new tweets are posted while your search results are on-screen, Twitter displays a banner to let you know.

Twitter keeps updating the banner, too. In the few minutes it took me to write the last couple of paragraphs, the banner updated itself (see Figure 6.4) to show me there were now 42 new tweets that matched my search!

6.4 For popular topics, the number of new tweets that match your search term can grow alarmingly fast.

Fortunately, Twitter is smart enough not to mess with your displayed search results, so you can continue to study them without interruption. However, if you're curious to see the very latest results, click the banner to rerun your search.

Performing Advanced Searches

A simple search on a word is often good enough to get a feel for what your fellow tweeters are saying about that topic, and you can often come across a few perfect posts that become immediate favorite candidates. (You can mark results as favorites in the new interface, as you learn later in this chapter.) However, if you want to really drill down into the depths of the Twitter database to unearth the true gems, then you need a more sophisticated approach. Here are some examples:

- Matching tweets that include a particular phrase or a particular collection of terms

- Matching tweets that don't include a particular word or phrase

- Searching for tweets posted by or replied to a person

- Restricting your search to tweets posted within a particular date range

- Searching for particular hashtags

You can perform all these types of searches and many more by using Twitter's advanced search features.

However, at this point you come to an interface fork in the road. The old Twitter interface includes an Advanced Search page that enables you to build fancy-schmancy search queries using familiar controls such as text boxes, lists, option buttons, and check boxes, as shown in Figure 6.5.

As of this writing, the new Twitter interface does not include the Advanced Search page as an integrated feature. You do have a couple of choices, however:

- You can still navigate to the Advanced Search page manually by typing the address http://search.twitter.com/advanced into your Web browser.

- Almost all the options in the Advanced Search page have equivalent search operators, such as the word OR for the Any of These Words text box, and the words "since" and "until" for date-related searches. These operators work in the new search interface, so you can build your advanced queries and get the better results provided by the new search engine. The downside to this approach is that you need to mess with more complex operator syntax rather than the nice Advanced Search controls.

So in the sections that follow I show you how to build each query using the Advanced Search form and using the equivalent search operators.

Performing an advanced word search

A simple word search is to look for tweets that match a single word. Advanced word searches include matching a phrase, matching multiple words in any order, matching one word or another, and matching tweets that exclude a word.

Advanced Search

Use this form to automatically construct your query. (Alternatively, you can type search operators directly into the search box.)

Find tweets based on...

| | Search |

Words		
	All of these words	
	This exact phrase	
	Any of these words	
	None of these words	
	This hashtag	
	Written in	English ▼ (persistent)
People	From this person	
	To this person	
	Referencing this person	
Places	Near this place	
	Within this distance	15 ▼ ◉ miles ◯ kilometers
Dates	Since this date	
	Until this date	
Attitudes	With positive attitude :)	☐

6.5 You can use the controls on the Advanced Search page to create sophisticated and powerful search queries.

Searching for tweets that include a phrase

If you want to search for a particular phrase, follow these steps to run the search using the Advanced Search form:

1. **Navigate to http://search.twitter.com/advanced.** The Advanced Search form appears.

2. **In the This exact phrase text box, type the phrase you want to match.**

3. **Click Search.** Twitter displays a list of tweets that contain the phrase.

However, this is one of those cases where it's easier and faster to not use the Advanced Search page. To search for tweets that match a phrase using the Search text box, enclose that phrase in quotation marks, as shown in Figure 6.6.

Real-time results for "craft beer" ⊕ Save this search

liquor mart LiquorMart RT @BoulderBeerCo: Featuring only extremely hard-to-find, high-quality **craft beer** from throughout the country, this ... http://bit.ly/6YkyuZ
21 minutes ago from HootSuite

BoulderBeerCo Featuring only extremely hard-to-find, high-quality **craft beer** from throughout the country, this is NOT your...
http://bit.ly/6YkyuZ
28 minutes ago from Facebook

Fr0sTy0nE I love not having a hangover after a heavy night of drinking. It's like a sign from God condoning my **craft beer** habit.
40 minutes ago from TwitBird iPhone

homemadebeer Motor City Brew Tours – Brewery Bus Tours - PR-USA.net: Newly launched Motor City Brew Tours offers **craft beer** fa... http://bit.ly/5ptFfd
about 1 hour ago from twitterfeed

Home
@paulmcf
Direct Messages   2
Favorites
Retweets

"craft beer"   🔍

Lists   ⊙
Trending Topics   ⊙
Following   ⊙

📶 RSS feed for this query

6.6 Place quotation marks around a phrase to match that phrase exactly within tweets or usernames.

Searching for tweets that include multiple words

If you want to look for tweets (or users) that contain multiple words in any order using the Advanced Search form, follow these steps:

1. **Navigate to http://search.twitter.com/advanced.** You see the Advanced Search page.

2. **In the All of these words text box, type each word you want to match.**

3. **Click Search.** Twitter displays a list of tweets that contain all of the words you typed.

Once again, this is another case where it's just easier to use the regular Search box. Just type the words you want to match into the Search box in any order, as shown in Figure 6.7.

Searching for tweets that include one word or another

You can also search for those tweets that include one or more words from a list of words. Here's how you do this using the Advanced Search form:

1. **Navigate to http://search.twitter.com/advanced.** The Advanced Search page appears.

2. **In the Any of these words text box, type the list of words from which you want Twitter to find its matches.** Remember that Twitter matches a tweet if it contains at least one of the words you type.

3. **Click Search.** Twitter displays a list of tweets that contain one or more of the words you typed.

Real-time results for imperial stout chocolate ⊕ Save this search

padschicago Sounds good! RT @DocJohnG: Southern Tier **Imperial** Mokah -- good **chocolate stout** beer. Yummy for dessert!
1 day ago from HootSuite

docjohng Southern Tier **Imperial** Mokah -- good **chocolate stout** beer. Yummy for dessert!
1 day ago from Seesmic

joefoodie Old Rasputin Russian **Imperial Stout**: bold, rich, & creamy. **Chocolate** & strong coffee with mild black licorice notes. Excellent #beer.
1 day ago from twidroid

nathanchantrell Couldn't resist the Durham Temptation... v. dark Russian **imperial stout**, quite sweet, lots of coffee, **chocolate** and strong on the liquorice.
1 day ago from Echofon

Home
@paulmcf
Direct Messages   2
Favorites
Retweets

imperial stout chocolate   🔍

Lists
Trending Topics
Following
RSS feed for this query

6.7 To match multiple terms, type the terms in any order.

You can also perform the same search using the Search box directly. As a bonus, you also get to search for those tweets that include one or more phrases from a list of phrases. The operator to use is the word OR (which you must use with all uppercase letters), and you insert it between each word or phrase (with the latter enclosed in quotation marks). Figure 6.8 shows an example and the results it generated.

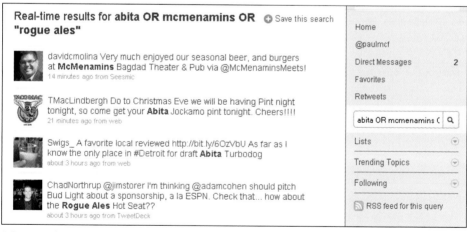

Real-time results for abita OR mcmenamins OR "rogue ales" ⊕ Save this search

davidcmolina Very much enjoyed our seasonal beer, and burgers at **McMenamins** Bagdad Theater & Pub via @McMenaminsMeets!
14 minutes ago from Seesmic

TMacLindbergh Do to Christmas Eve we will be having Pint night tonight, so come get your **Abita** Jockamo pint tonight. Cheers!!!!
21 minutes ago from web

Swigs_ A favorite local reviewed http://bit.ly/6OzVbU As far as I know the only place in #Detroit for draft **Abita** Turbodog
about 3 hours ago from web

ChadNorthrup @jimstorer I'm thinking @adamcohen should pitch Bud Light about a sponsorship, a la ESPN. Check that... how about the **Rogue Ales** Hot Seat??
about 3 hours ago from TweetDeck

Home
@paulmcf
Direct Messages   2
Favorites
Retweets

abita OR mcmenamins O   🔍

Lists
Trending Topics
Following
RSS feed for this query

6.8 To match one or more items from a list of words and phrases, separate each item with the search operator OR.

Searching for tweets that exclude a word

It's often useful to search for tweets that don't include a particular word. For example, if you're interested in pale ale but you don't want to investigate the IPA (India pale ale) variety, you can tell

Twitter to skip tweets that include the term "IPA." Here's how it's done using the Advanced Search page:

1. **Navigate to http://search.twitter.com/advanced.** The Advanced Search form loads.
2. **In the None of these words text box, type one or more words that you want to use to exclude tweets.**
3. **Click Search.** Twitter displays a list of tweets that don't contain the words you typed.

You can run the same type of search using the Search box directly, but you can also search for those tweets that exclude the phrases you specify. The operator you use is the minus sign (-), and you insert it immediately in front of the word or phrase you want excluded from the matching tweets. (For a phrase, note that you must put the minus sign inside the quotation marks.) Figure 6.9 shows an example and its results.

6.9 To match those tweets that don't include a particular word or phrase, place a minus sign (-) in front of that word or phrase (within the quotation marks for the latter).

Running an advanced people search

Although most of your Twitter searching expeditions will scour tweet text for matching posts, it's also useful to search based on people. For example, you might want to see all the posts sent by a user, all the posts sent to a user, or all the posts that mention a particular user. You perform these people-related searches using either the Advanced Search form or the Search box.

Searching for tweets from a person

If you want to see all the tweets that someone has posted, it's easiest to navigate to that person's profile page on Twitter. However, what if you want to see only some subsets of those tweets? For example, you might want to see only those tweets that include a certain word or phrase. For that, you need to take it up a notch and construct a search engine query.

Here's how you can search for tweets posted by someone using the Advanced Search page:

1. **Navigate to http://search.twitter.com/advanced.** The Advanced Search page appears.

2. **In the From this person text box, type the Twitter username of the person whose tweets you want to search.**

3. **Use one or more of the text boxes in the Words section to specify which tweets you want to match.**

4. **Click Search.** Twitter displays a list of tweets from that person that match your other criteria.

You can also search for a person's tweets from the Search box. The operator you use is from:, and you insert it immediately in front of the username. In Figure 6.10, I've constructed (and run) a search query that looks for posts from the user allbeernews that contain the word *craft*.

6.10 To return the tweets posted by a user, precede that person's username with from:.

Searching for replies to a person

Twitter replies are elusive creatures because you only see them on certain occasions:

- If the reply is sent to you

- If the reply is sent by someone you follow to someone you follow

However, replies are public for most users, so it seems reasonable that there be some way to get at them. If you want to search the replies sent to a particular person, then you need to use the search engine, which also gives you the added benefit of being able to filter the result based on other search terms.

Here's how to search the replies sent to a person using the Advanced Search page:

1. **Navigate to http://search.twitter.com/advanced to display the Advanced Search form.**
2. **In the To this person text box, type the Twitter username of the person whose received replies you want to search.**
3. **Use one or more of the text boxes in the Words section to specify which tweets you want to match.**
4. **Click Search.** Twitter displays a list of replies sent to that person that match your other criteria.

To search for the replies sent to a person from the Search box, use the to: operator, which you insert immediately in front of the username. In Figure 6.11, I've built a search query that looks for replies to the user grahamfarmelo (who wrote a terrific biography of the physicist Paul Dirac) that contain the word *Dirac*.

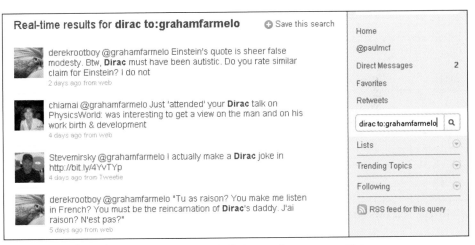

6.11 To return the replies sent to a user, precede that person's username with to:.

Searching for tweets that mention a person

Reply tweets always begin with @*username*, but plenty of tweets mention users by including @*username* somewhere within the tweet text. It could be a retweet, a shout-out to someone, an acknowledgment of an original post, a FollowFriday recommendation, or whatever. For these types of tweets, you can search for updates that include a reference to a user, possibly also filtered with other search criteria.

To search for tweets that mention a user with the Advanced Search page, follow these steps:

1. **Navigate to http://search.twitter.com/advanced.** The Advanced Search page appears.

2. **In the Referencing this person text box, type the Twitter username of the person whose mentions you want to search.**

3. **Use one or more of the text boxes in the Words section to specify which tweets you want to match.**

4. **Click Search.** Twitter displays a list of tweets that mention the person and that match your other criteria.

To search for a user's mentions from the Search box, use the @ operator, which you insert immediately in front of the username. In Figure 6.12, I've put together a search query that looks for mentions of the user wordspy that contain the text RT (so they're old-style retweets).

6.12 To return the tweets that mention a user, precede that person's username with @.

Filtering tweets by hashtag

You can tag a post with a particular topic by including in the tweet the topic word preceded by the hash symbol (#). For example, if you post a tweet related to Microsoft's Windows 7 operating system, you could include the hashtag #windows7 somewhere in the tweet. However, the real purpose behind hashtagging tweets is that they give you and other tweeters an easy way to search for a particular topic because the hashtag acts as a kind of natural filter.

Here's how to perform a hashtag search using the Advanced Search page:

1. **Navigate to http://search.twitter.com/advanced.** The Advanced Search form appears.
2. **In the This hashtag text box, type the hashtag topic you want to find.** Don't add the hash (#) in front of the topic word; Twitter adds it for you automatically.
3. **Click Search.** You see a list of tweets that include the hashtag.

Hashtag searching is probably easiest from the Search box because all you have to do is place the hashtag operator (#) in front of the topic. For example, Figure 6.13 shows a search for the hashtag #blackberry where the tweet also includes the sad emoticon :(.

Real-time results for #blackberry :(⊕ Save this search

Jaineen Im not having a good **#blackberry** day today :(
33 minutes ago from HootSuite

aleksandra94 Why is **#BlackBerry** TT?? :P
about 1 hour ago from Seesmic

anikakhan I miss my **#blackberry** :(
about 2 hours ago from TwitBird iPhone

maniac_rare **#BlackBerry** is a trending topic?!? my ubertwitter isn't
workinggggg :(http://bit.ly/7lFm41
about 2 hours ago from TweetGrid

hii_heartache **#BlackBerry** is a trending topic?!? my ubertwitter
isn't workinggggg :(
about 2 hours ago from web

Home
@paulmcf
Direct Messages   2
Favorites
Retweets

#blackberry :(🔍

Lists
Trending Topics
Following

📶 RSS feed for this query

6.13 To locate the tweets that include a particular topic, precede the topic word with #.

If you want to search for happy tweets, include the classic smiley in your search string :).
If you're using the Advanced Search form, you can include the :) and :(operators by
selecting the With positive attitude and With negative attitude check boxes, respectively.

Searching for tweets by location

If you use a Twitter client on a mobile device that includes a global positioning system (GPS) sensor, chances are that the client can use that information to update your Twitter location information. For example, the iPhone clients TweetDeck, Twittelator Pro, Tweetie, and Twitterific can all take advantage of the GPS sensor in the iPhone 3G and 3GS. Tweets you send are tagged with your current position, so many Twitter updates have an associated location. (For tweets from people who haven't specified their location or who've used some vague or jokey location, this information isn't so useful.)

If you're interested in locating people who are tweeting near a particular location, you can use Twitter Search to specify that location as well as a distance. For example, you could search for tweets that were sent within 10 miles of Kalamazoo, Michigan.

Here are the steps to follow to search for tweets by location using the Advanced Search page:

1. **Navigate to http://search.twitter.com/advanced.** The Advanced Search form appears.
2. **In the Near this place text box, type the location.**
3. **Use the Within this distance list to select a value.** The choices are 1, 5, 10, 15, 25, 50, 100, 500, or 1000.
4. **Select either miles or kilometers.**
5. **Click Search.** Twitter displays a list of tweets that were sent within the specified distance of the location.

To perform location-based searches from the Search box, you use two operators:

- **near:** Use this operator followed by a place name to search for tweets sent from that location.
- **within:** Use this operator followed by a number followed by either mi (for miles) or km (for kilometers) to search for tweets within that distance of the location.

One advantage you get with using these operators is that you can use them on their own. For example, using near: on its own returns all the posts sent from just that location. Similarly, using within: on its own returns all the posts sent within the specified distance of your current location.

Figure 6.14 shows a search query that looks for posts sent within 10 miles of Portland, and I've also added the search term brewpub.

finding tweets by date

I mentioned at the beginning of this chapter that more than 5 billion tweets have been posted, but it's a sad fact of Twitter life that the vast majority of those 5 billion updates are invisible to the Twitter search engine. That's because Twitter Search refuses to return any results that are more than a week old! That fits with Twitter's relentless focus on "What's happening?" (meaning, really, "What's happening *now*?").

You learn how to search for older tweets a bit later in this chapter, but for now you're stuck searching a week's worth of Twitter data. That's not as limiting as you might imagine because if there's some major event or breaking story going on, you probably don't need to know what people were saying about the topic six months ago; you want to know what people have said about the topic lately.

Real-time results for brewpub near:portland within:10mi ⊕ Save this search

bill_of_lading eating and drinking at PDX airport has improved immensely since the opening of Laurelhurst **Brewpub**. Enjoying pulled pork and Free Range Red.
about 19 hours ago from web

portlandbarfly Added listing info for The Workshop **Brewpub** #pdxdrinks http://pdx.be/yus
about 19 hours ago from API

airportbars @mickie00 SLC has a few bars, hope this helps: http://www.airportbars.com/bars/SLC/ The **brewpub** is very popular.
about 22 hours ago from web

bryanrhoads 2010 Strategy w/ @kellyrfeller (@ BridgePort **Brewpub**) http://4sq.com/4XJpuT
about 23 hours ago from foursquare

Home
@paulmcf
Direct Messages   2
Favorites
Retweets
brewpub near:portland w   🔍
Lists   ⊙
Trending Topics   ⊙
Following   ⊙
📶 RSS feed for this query

6.14 To return tweets based on location, precede that location with near: and optionally also specify a distance using the within: operator.

The real problem is that Twitter sorts search results chronologically, so for a popular or relevant topic, the tweets you're most interested in might be simply too far back in the results. To fix that, you can specify the tweet dates you want to see in the search results. You can specify a start date and an end date.

Follow these steps to search for tweets by date using the Advanced Search page:

1. **Navigate to http://search.twitter.com/advanced.** The Advanced Search page appears.

2. **In the Since this date text box, type the start date.** Use the format yyyy-mm-dd. You can also click the calendar icon and choose the date from the calendar that pops up.

3. **In the Until this date text box, type the end date.** Again, use the format yyyy-mm-dd, or click the calendar icon.

4. **Type your other search criteria, as needed.**

5. **Click Search.** Twitter displays a list of tweets that were sent within the specified distance of the location.

To perform date-based searches using the handy Search box, you need to familiarize yourself with two operators:

- **since:** Use this operator followed by a date in the yyyy-mm-dd format to specify the start date.

- **until:** Use this operator followed by a date in the yyyy-mm-dd format to specify the end date.

You can use each operator on its own to restrict the search results on one end only, or you can use them together to set a date range.

To restrict the search results to a specific date, use the same date with both the since: operator and the until: operator.

In Figure 6.15, I've cobbled together a search query that looks for tweets that mention the phrase *winter solstice* on December 21, 2009.

Real-time results for "winter solstice" since:2009-12-20 until:2009-12-21

Save this search

nordicheart @stran9ee December 21st is always the start of winter by the **winter solstice** time.
Dec 21, 2009 10:59 PM GMT from Echofon

tomvell **Winter Solstice** live tweets - http://avoo.net/kiyxf
Dec 21, 2009 10:59 PM GMT from API

meadowgirl mmm roasted chicken, mashed potatoes, salad and carrots for **Winter Solstice**!
Dec 21, 2009 10:59 PM GMT from web

AMORC Rosicrucians Celebrate the **Winter Solstice** with the Festival of Light http://bit.ly/4GBjla
Dec 21, 2009 10:59 PM GMT from Facebook

Home
@paulmcf
Direct Messages   2
Favorites
Retweets

"winter solstice" since:20   🔍

Lists
Trending Topics
Following
RSS feed for this query

6.15 To return tweets based on the date they were sent, precede the start date with the since: operator, and precede the end date with the until: operator.

Locating tweets that contain links

For many Twitter fans, the most important tweets are the ones that contain links to other sites because they're often the most interesting, the most useful, or the most fun. So it's great that the Twitter search engine includes an option that lets you specify that it should only return tweets that contain links.

Here's how to use this option from the Advanced Search page:

1. **Navigate to http://search.twitter.com/advanced.** The Advanced Search form appears.
2. **Select the Containing Links check box.**
3. **Type your other search criteria.**

4. **Click Search.** Twitter returns only those tweets that have at least one link.

To get your Search box-based searching to return only tweets with links, include filter:links as part of your search string. Figure 6.16 shows an example where I've searched on the word *hilarious* and included filter:links to hopefully find some links to fun things.

6.16 To return only tweets with links, add filter:links to your search query.

Adding Twitter Search to Your Web Browser

If you use Internet Explorer 7 or 8, or Firefox (or indeed, any Web browser that supports OpenSearch; alas, Safari does not), you can configure the browser's Search box to include Twitter Search. After you do that, you can type your search query in the browser and it passes it along to Twitter.

Adding Twitter Search to Internet Explorer

By default, Internet Explorer's Search box uses the Bing search engine. If you want to get Twitter in there, you need to create what's called a *custom search provider*. Here are the steps to follow:

1. **Navigate to the Twitter search page at http://search.twitter.com/.**
2. **Run a search using TEST (all caps) as the search string.**
3. **Copy the resulting URL from the Address bar.**

4. **Click the drop-down arrow to the right of the Search box, and then click Find More Providers.** Internet Explorer displays a list of search providers.

5. **Scroll to the bottom of the window and click the Create your own Search Provider link.** The Create your own Search Provider page appears.

6. **Click inside the URL text box and paste the address from Step 3.**

7. **Use the Name text box to specify the name you want to appear in the Search box list (such as "Twitter").** Figure 6.17 shows an example that's ready to go.

6.17 Use the Create your own Search Provider page to create a custom search provider for Twitter.

8. **Click Install Search Provider.** The Add Search Provider dialog box appears.

9. **If you want Internet Explorer to use Twitter as the default search engine, select the Make this My Default Search Provider check box.**

10. **Click Add.** Internet Explorer adds Twitter to the list of search engines.

To use Twitter within Internet Explorer, pull down the Search box list, and click Twitter (or whatever you name your custom search provider). Type a search query and press Enter, and Internet Explorer displays the results in Twitter, as shown in Figure 6.18.

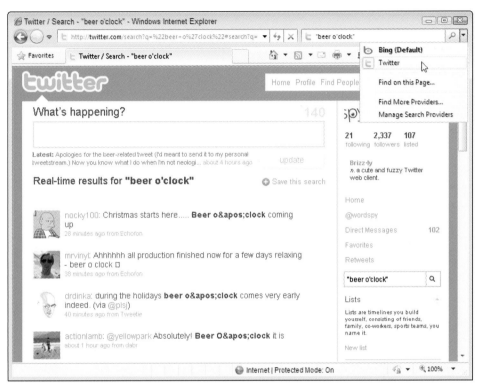

6.18 Internet Explorer customized to include Twitter in the Search box

Adding Twitter Search to Firefox

Adding Twitter Search to the Firebox Search box is quite a bit easier than with Internet Explorer. Here's all you have to do:

1. **Navigate to the Twitter search page at http://search.twitter.com/.**

2. **Pull down the Search box menu, as shown in Figure 6.19.**

3. **Click Add "Twitter Search."** Firefox adds Twitter Search to its list of search engines. Now that was easy!

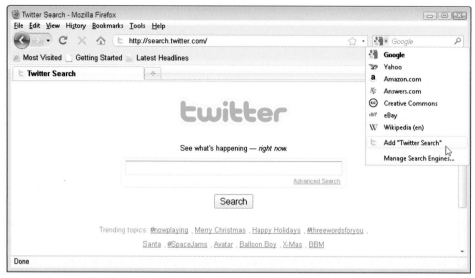

6.19 To configure Firefox to use Twitter Search, choose the Add "Twitter Search" command on the Search box menu.

Working with Search Results

Once your search results are arrayed before you, it's just a matter of scrolling through the tweets, looking for the information you want, trying to find something that catches your eye, or just getting a feel for "What's happening?" in that particular slice of the Twitter pie. There are seven basic things you can do with individual search results:

⦿ **Save the search for later use by clicking the Save this Search link.** Twitter creates a Saved Searches section in your sidebar and adds a link to the search query.

 If you no longer want a particular search to appear in the Saved Searches area, click the search to run it one last time, and then click the Remove this Saved Search link.

⦿ **Reply to a result by hovering your mouse over the tweet in the search results and then clicking the Reply icon (the arrow).**

⦿ **Retweet a result by hovering your mouse over the tweet in the search results and then clicking the Retweet icon (the double arrows).**

⦿ **Mark a result as a favorite by hovering the mouse pointer over the tweet in the search results and then clicking the Favorite icon (the star).**

- **Check out the tweeter's profile page by clicking the username at the beginning of the tweet or by clicking the avatar to the left of the tweet.**

- **Click a tweet's link (if it has one) to visit the site.**

- **See the archive version of the tweet.** In the new search interface, you do this by clicking the "about *time* ago" link under the tweet (where *time* is a time value such as "10 minutes" or "3 hours").

Using a feed to monitor search results

Some searches are one-time-only deals where you run your search, check the results, and then return to whatever you were doing. Sometimes, however, you want to run the same search frequently. For example, you might want to know whenever a tweeter talks about a particular product or service, your company, or yourself. (Don't worry, everyone searches for themselves on Twitter; call it *egoTwittering*.) In those cases, it would sure be nice to have some way to monitor the search results.

I mentioned earlier that Twitter monitors your current search query in the background and kindly lets you know if new tweets that match your query show up. That's fine as long as you have the Twitter search results displayed, which these days isn't all that inconvenient because all the major Web browsers support tabbed browsing, so you can leave your search open in a tab while you move on with other things.

Of course, you'll eventually close that browser session or turn off or reboot your computer, so the next time you're back in the Twitterverse you'll have to run the same search again. To avoid that, a better monitoring idea is to create a feed for the search, which will let you monitor the search from the friendly confines of your favorite feed reader, such as Google Reader, NewsGator, or Bloglines.

If you're a TweetDeck user, you can also monitor a Twitter search within the TweetDeck window. See Chapter 8 for the full scoop.

Fortunately, creating that feed is just a click away because Twitter displays with each batch of search results an RSS feed for this query link at the bottom of the sidebar. Click that link, and when the feed page opens copy the URL from the Address bar. Now switch to your feed reader, create a new subscription, and paste the address when the feed reader asks you for the feed URL.

Rather than opening the feed in your browser, right-click (or Ctrl+click on your Mac) Twitter's feed link on the results page, and then click Copy Shortcut (if you're using Internet Explorer), Copy Link Location (Firefox), or Copy Link (Safari).

Sending your search results as a tweet

When you're searching the Twitter landscape, you might come upon some sight or landmark that's particularly striking, so much so that you want to share your discovery with the people who follow you. That's very nice of you. Here's how you do it:

1. **Run the search.**

2. **Copy the resulting URL from the browser's Address bar.**

3. **Click Home to return to your Twitter home page.**

4. **Paste the URL into the What's happening? box.**

5. **Type a short message that describes the search.** If you want to include the search query, click your browser's Back button, copy the search text, click your browser's Forward button, and then paste the string into the update box.

6. **Click Update.**

If by including the full URL in your tweet you go over the 140-character limit, you need to shorten the URL. See Chapter 9 for some pointers to some URL-shortening services that are available.

Twitter Search Engines and Tools

Recent improvements to Twitter's search engine show the newfound importance of search to the Twitter powers that be. However, there's another sign that mining Twitter for tweet gold is becoming a big thing: the existence of a large and ever-increasing collection of Web sites that extend and enhance Twitter Search.

There's a kind of gold rush feel to all this as companies recognize a great opportunity: Twitter is going mainstream, for sure, and Twitter Search itself is merely okay, so there's a fantastic chance to become the de facto Twitter search engine. The result is a slew of Twitter-related search sites and tools. There are way too many to list here, so instead I'll just run through the ones I use most often, which are covered in no particular order.

As usual, the best place to keep track of the latest additions to the Twitter search collection is the Twitter Fan Wiki: http://twitter.pbworks.com/Search.

Bing

Of the major search engines, Microsoft's Bing was the first to officially get its Web-crawling mitts on Twitter's vast tweet database, and it has come up with a new and innovative way to display tweet search results. To get started, point your Web browser here:

```
http://www.bing.com/twitter/
```

Type a search term in the search box and press Enter. Figure 6.20 shows an example results page.

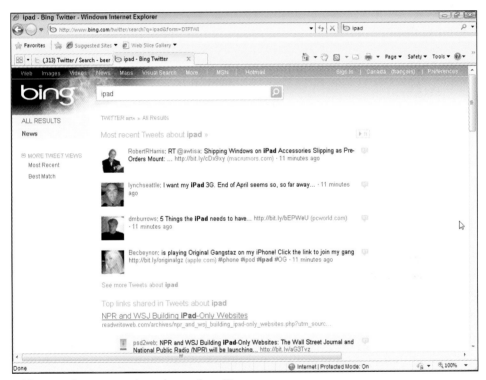

6.20 A typical Twitter search result page from Bing

Like Twitter itself, Bing is relentlessly focused on the recent, so you never see results that are more than a week old.

There's actually a lot going on here, so let's go through everything that Bing brings to the Twitter search table:

- The first part of the search results has the heading Most recent Tweets about *query*, where *query* is the search term you typed. Below that heading you see the four most recent tweets that match your search.

- The Most recent Tweets section is "live" in the sense that if another tweet comes along while you're examining the results, Bing will display the tweet. If you'd prefer not to see results as they come in, click the Pause button.

- If a recent tweet includes a shortened URL, Bing displays the actual domain name of the destination link in green text beside the shortened URL. (This is a welcome feature because it means you always know where the link will take you, which can be a real problem with shortened URLs, as I discuss in Chapter 9.)

- The second part of the search results has the heading Top links shared in Tweets about *query*, where *query* is your search text. Below that heading you see the most popular links to sites that match your search.

- All tweet results include an RT icon, which enables you to retweet (in the old fashioned "RT" style) a result.

- Below the Most recent Tweets section you see a See more Tweets about *query* link, where *query* is your search term. This shows you a longer list of recent tweets that is, at first, sorted chronologically (with the most recent tweets at the top, of course). However, you can also click the Best Match link, which sorts the tweets by relevance (see Figure 6.21). Here, "relevance" usually means that tweets from folks with more followers get ranked higher, as do tweets that are unique (that is, that haven't been repeated ad nauseam).

Google

As the Web's de facto default search engine, it's only natural that we should turn to the almighty Google to search for tweets. First, note that Google does seem to have indexed a big chunk of Twitter's database of 5 billion tweets. To query that database, run a Google search that uses the following general format:

```
site:twitter.com query
```

Here, replace *query* with the search text you want Google to match. For example, Figure 6.22 shows the results of a Google search on the phrase "just setting up my twttr," which is famously the first-ever Twitter update, and it was tweeted by Twitter co-founder Jack Dorsey. (And, as you can see in Figure 6.22, it's an oft-imitated line.) Clicking the link takes you to the original tweet, which, as you can see in Figure 6.23, was posted on March 21, 2006.

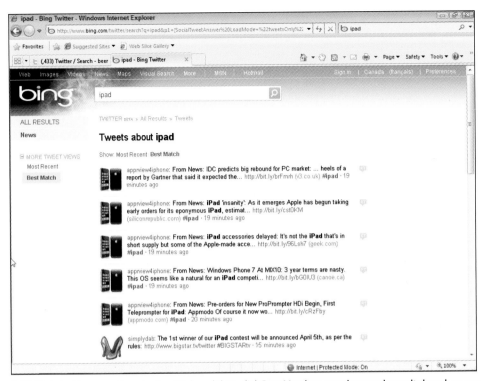

6.21 Click the See more Tweets about link and then click Best Match to sort the search results by relevance.

6.22 Add site:twitter.com to your Google searches to return results only from the Twitter site.

6.23 The first tweet ever posted to Twitter

 note Why does Jack Dorsey refer to "twttr" instead of "Twitter"? Because, believe it or not, twttr was the original name of the service! Fortunately, saner heads prevailed and the vowel-challenged version was dropped. Whew!

However, if Twitter is all about what's happening now, then who cares about some dusty, old tweets? Can Google follow Bing's lead and show us those up-to-the-minute search results that we crave? Why, yes, it can. Here's how:

1. **Go to www.google.com/ and run a search on the term you want to research.** Google displays the results for the entire Web.

2. **Click the Show options link.** Google displays its search options to the left of the results.

3. **Click Latest.** Google displays the most recent results from sites such as blogs and forums.

4. **Click Updates.** Google filters the results to show just those from Twitter, as shown in Figure 6.24.

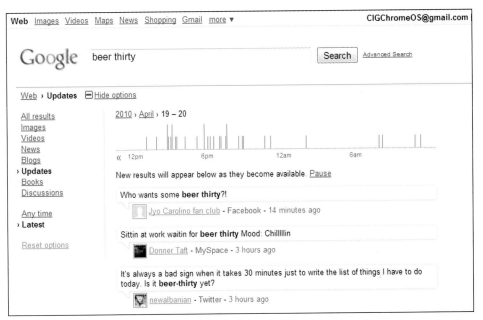

6.24 In the Google options sidebar, click Latest and then click Updates to see the most recent tweets that match your search query.

Note that the results are "live" in the sense that if another tweet comes along while you're examining the results, Google will display the tweet. If you'd prefer not to see results as they come in, click the Pause link.

As this edition was going to press, Google announced that it would soon include the entire Twitter database in the Updates category, not just the past week. Use the timeline that appears at the top of the results (see Figure 6.24) to choose the timeframe of your search.

Tweet Scan

When I'm in a simple mood (a not uncommon occurrence), I prefer to deal with sites that offer simple, uncluttered interfaces with nary a bell or whistle in view. For searching Twitter, the simple site I like is Tweet Scan (http://tweetscan.com/). As you can see in Figure 6.25, Tweet Scan's home page includes just a humble text box for your search string (which supports the standard Twitter search operators), plus a tag cloud that shows the most popular Twitter topics. (The larger and more bold the type, the more popular the topic.) Search results are automatically refreshed every 90 seconds, you can reply to tweeters, and you can post the results as a tweet.

TWEET**SCAN**

| | Search |

Search Cloud:

#oeb2009 #schweitzer 79.9% @PaulaAbdul EWE NaturWatt Gospel Music
Smashing Magazine UPC Vattenfall natur Venceslau bbm bradesco
breathtaking broche caregiver caregiving christmas debt ews schönau
firefox gym itau ivf-embryo journotwit justinvincent kmilo michael buble new years obama why
openid photo real estate recruiter jobs rurihimura sellos seo sex shanghai sj39 sticker strasserauf
theaarondouglas upskirt venganza web analytics

What is this? Sign in Find People Download Sterry IT, LLC

6.25 Tweet Scan offers a straightforward interface for searching Twitter.

Twitterfall

When I'm in a complex mood (rare!), I don't mind navigating sites that are festooned with options, settings, links, and other bric-a-brac. When it comes to third-party Twitter searching, perhaps the champion site for complexity is Twitterfall (http://twitterfall.com/), which shows real-time, constantly updated results for one or more search terms. The "fall" part of Twitterfall refers to the animation the site uses: As a new result appears, the existing results slide down the page.

To run your own search, type a term in the text box in the Searches area, and then click Add. You're free to create multiple searches, and you can turn individual searches on and off using check boxes.

Figure 6.26 shows Twitterfall with two custom searches running: one for "craft beer" and another for "extreme beer." Notice that when you hover your mouse over a tweet, the fall pauses and you see a collection of icons to the right of the tweet. If you're logged in to your Twitter account, you can use these icons to reply to the tweeter, send a direct message to the user (if you're mutual followers), retweet or favorite the update, follow the user, and view the tweet in Twitter.

TweetGrid

If you want to monitor multiple search queries, you could set up each one as a feed in your feed reader, which is fine for results that don't change much. However, if you want to monitor these results in real time and you want Twitter interactivity such as sending replies and marking favorites, your feed reader would have no idea what you're talking about.

6.26 Twitterfall offers multiple real-time search results with lots of options for each tweet.

Instead, I highly recommend a great site called TweetGrid (http://tweetgrid.com/). The "grid" part of the name means that you can display multiple Twitter searches, each of which appears in its own box, and those boxes are arranged in a grid. Several grid structures are available, such as 1×1 (a single search), 1×2 (two searches arranged in a single row with two columns), 2×3 (six searches arranged in two rows and three columns), and more. In each box you get a text box to type your search string (you can use the standard Twitter search operators), and a Search! button to click to start the search. Figure 6.27 shows TweetGrid with a 2×3 grid running six different searches, all updating on the fly!

TweetGrid also lets you interact with Twitter. Type your username and password in the User and Pass text boxes, respectively, and TweetGrid uses that data whenever you want to exchange data with Twitter. For example, hover your mouse over a tweet and several icons appear in the lower-right corner of the tweet. (In Figure 6.27, you see these icons in the first tweet of the top-left box in the grid.) These icons enable you to reply, retweet, or favorite the tweet, send a direct message to the tweeter (if you're mutual followers), view the tweet in the Twitter archive, and send the tweet via e-mail. You can also use TweetGrid to send a tweet.

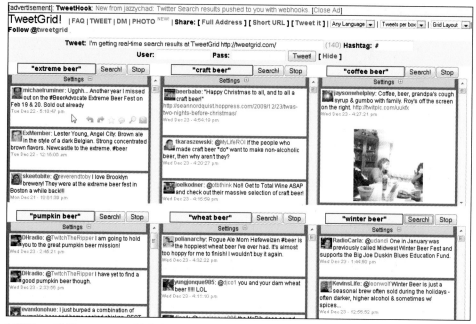

6.27 TweetGrid arranges multiple Twitter searches in a grid.

 You can't save your TweetGrid layout, but you can add it as a bookmark in your Web browser. Right-click (or Ctrl+click on your Mac) the Full Address link, and then click Add to Favorites (if you're using Internet Explorer), Bookmark This Link (Firefox), or Add Link to Bookmarks (Safari).

Monitter

If your Twitter searching is all about location, location, location, you could add the near: and within: operators to your search queries. However, an easier way is to use Monitter (http://monitter.com/). This site lets you define multiple search queries, and the results of each query are displayed in a column. More importantly for location fans, you can filter all the results using distance and location, as shown in Figure 6.28. For each tweet you get links to reply, retweet, or view the tweeter's profile, plus you see the tweeter's location.

TweetBeep

Have you ever used Google Alerts, the service that sends you daily or weekly Google search results? It's an incredibly useful service, and if you've ever wished you could get the same convenience with Twitter, wish no more. With TweetBeep (http://tweetbeep.com/), you can define a Twitter search query, and then TweetBeep sends you a daily or even an hourly e-mail alert with the latest results.

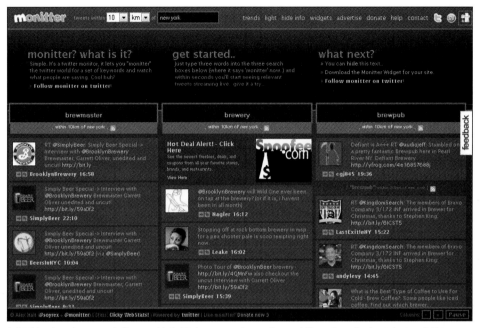

6.28 Monitter lets you define multiple Twitter search queries and filter them by location and distance.

After you create a TweetBeep account, you can immediately start creating alerts (although TweetBeep won't send you any alerts until you confirm your account by clicking the link in the e-mail message it sends you). Click My Alerts, and then click New Keyword Alert to display the New Keyword Alert page, as shown in Figure 6.29. The layout of this page is nearly identical to Twitter's Advanced Search form. Fill in the fields to define your search criteria, click Save Alert, and then sit back and let TweetBeep do all the work.

One of TweetBeep's sweetest features is the domain alert, which looks for domain names in tweet links, and it can even sniff out domains from shortened URLs. It's a great way to find out when a tweeter mentions your Web site. Click New Domain Alert, type your domain name, and then click Save Alert.

Twemes

Hashtags are an easy way to track tweet topics, and you can use the hash (#) operator to search for a tag using Twitter Search. However, that only scratches the surface of the surface when it comes to hashtags. To delve deeper into this powerful tool, check out Twemes (http://twemes.com/), which specializes in viewing and searching hashtags. The Twemes (the name is a mashup of *Twitter* and *memes*) home page shows you a list of hashtags that have been recently updated, as well as a hashtag cloud (bigger and bolder means more popular).

tweet**beep**))

TweetBeep
is like
Google Alerts
for Twitter!

New Keyword Alert

Settings

Alert Name | Twitter Tips

Alert Frequency | Every Hour ▾

Keywords

All of these words | twitter

This exact phrase |

Any of these words | tips tricks

None of these words |

This hashtag |

Written in | English ▾

6.29 Use this page to define your Twitter search query, and then TweetBeep sends you hourly or daily results via e-mail.

> One quirk of the Twemes site is that it uses the word *tweme* instead of *hashtag*. Just remember that whenever the site talks about a tweme, it's really talking about a hashtag.

note

You can also search for a hashtag by typing a topic (without the #) in the search box and clicking search. In the search results, click start live update to follow the hashtag in real time (see Figure 6.30).

AskTwitR

AskTwitR (http://asktwitr.com/) is a very basic Twitter search engine with one unique feature that makes it just a bit addictive: When you run a Twitter search from the simple home page, the first thing you see on the results page is a Google map. Within seconds, locations start popping up on the map, each of which is a tweet from the search results (see Figure 6.31). Each pop-up shows the tweet text and the tweeter's avatar, and the pointer shows you the user's location on the map. It's oddly mesmerizing. Scroll down (if you can drag yourself away from the map) and you see matching Flickr photos, matching YouTube photos, and then (finally) the matching tweets.

6.30 Using the Twemes site, you can search for a hashtag and then display real-time results.

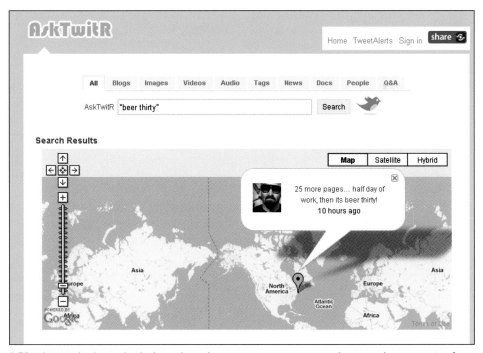

6.31 AskTwitR displays individual search results on a map so you can see where people are tweeting from.

BackTweets

If you want to see who has mentioned your Web site on Twitter, you could simply enter *domain*.com as a Twitter search (where *domain* is your domain name). However, the results miss all those links to your site that have been cut down to size with a URL-shortening service. (And because most addresses on Twitter are shortened, you'll miss a lot of tweets!) A better approach is to let BackTweets (http://backtweets.com/) handle this for you. You type the address you want to search — it could be a simple domain name, a partial address, or a full URL— and click Search. BackTweets looks in the Twitter links for the address text you specified, and then displays the matching tweets. Best of all, it can even ferret out the address within a shortened URL (see Figure 6.32), so you won't miss a mention.

6.32 BackTweets can find addresses in tweet links, even if those links use shortened URLs.

TweetVolume

If you're researching a topic, it's often useful to run Google searches on different words and then compare the number of results that Google finds. If one term is vastly more popular than another, then you might decide to use the more popular term in a post or a marketing campaign.

For example, when I began writing this book, I couldn't decide how to refer to people who use Twitter: Tweeters? Tweeple? Twitterers? Tweople? Tweeps? For the most part, I use *tweeters*, if only because *Twitterers* is hard to say, and *tweeple* is a plural-only term.

However, what I should have done is use TweetVolume (http://tweetvolume.com/) to research each term within Twitter. TweetVolume is very simple: You type up to five search terms, and the site returns the number of matching tweets, all displayed in a nice bar graph for easy comparison. Figure 6.33 shows the results for my five Twitter user terms. As you can see, *tweeters* is the winner!

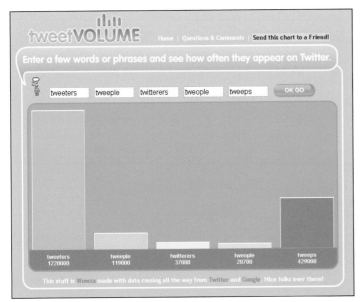

6.33 Use TweetVolume to compare the number of hits garnered by up to five search terms.

Where Can I Display My Twitter Feed?

1 2 3 4 5 6 7 8 9

It's a rare Twitter user who doesn't want to have more followers. Few of us can aspire to the Olympian heights of the Twitterati and their millions of followers, but getting your count up to a few dozen or even a few hundred sure helps you get motivated to tweet. Good content drives up your followership, but how do you get people to see your content? In this chapter, you learn about two techniques that help: augmenting your regular Web site with links to your Twitter profile, and displaying your Twitter feed on your social-networking site or Web site.

Adding Twitter Bling to Your Web Site

Now that you're well established on Twitter and you're tweeting away with your 140-characters-or-less observations, ideas, and updates, it's time to fly your Twitter flag. If you have a blog, personal home page, or other Web site where you live your online life outside of Twitter, you should dress up that site with text or image links that take people to your Twitter home page. If people like what they see and use Twitter, they need only click your Follow button to get onboard; if they're not on Twitter yet, you might just inspire them to get an account so they can keep up with your tweets. Either way, you end up with more followers and life just keeps getting better.

Adding a Twitter link to your Web site

The simplest way to point someone to your tweets is to add a link to your Twitter home page. Ideally, you should place this link near the top of your page where people are sure to see it. Most sites have content that automatically appears on every page (such as a site header or a sidebar), and that's the ideal location because it means you only have to add the link once to that section and it appears automatically on all your other pages.

Creating a text link

If your Web host provides you with an online editor, use it to insert your links. How this works varies from host to host, but the following general steps are nearly the same with all hosts: Place the cursor where you want the link to appear and add some text (for example, "Follow Me on Twitter" or "See What I'm Doing on Twitter"). Select the text, click the editor's link tool, and then specify the address http://twitter.com/*yourname*, where *yourname* is your Twitter username.

If your site requires you to edit HTML to add a link, open the page or file in your HTML editor, place the cursor where you want the link to appear, and then type the link using the following HTML code (replace *yourname* with your Twitter username, and modify the link text to suit your style):

```
<a href="http://twitter.com/yourname">Follow me on Twitter!</a>
```

Creating a Twitter badge link

A humble text link is better than nothing, I suppose, but if it's Twitter bling you want on your site, then plain text just doesn't cut it. Instead, you need to get yourself a Twitter *badge* (also called a *button*), a small graphic that includes something Twitterish (such as a bird or some variation on the Twitter logo), which you then set up as a link to your Twitter home page.

Your first task is to locate a Twitter badge that you like. Here are some sites to check out:

- **Twitter.** http://twitter.com/goodies/buttons

- **Limeshot Design.** http://limeshot.com/2008/follow-me-on-twitter-badges

- **Randa Clay Design.** http://randaclay.com/freebies/free-twitter-graphics/

- **Shia Design.** http://siahdesign.com/archives/150

- **Vincent Abry.** www.vincentabry.com/31-logos-et-boutons-pour-twitter-2480

Figure 7.1 shows the badges available on the Twitter site.

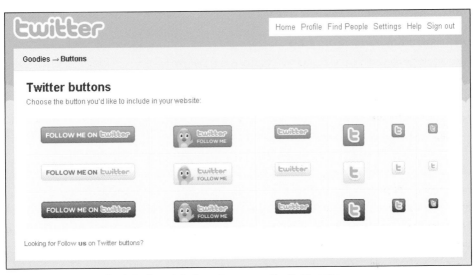

7.1 You can get some basic badges right from the source: the Twitter site.

Twitter's badges say "Follow Me" by default. To get a "Follow Us" badge, instead, click the Follow us on Twitter link below the badges.

Note that it's considered bad form to link directly to a badge on another site. Instead, you should download the badge you want to use to your computer, and then upload the file to your own Web site. Here are the instructions for using Internet Explorer, Firefox, and Safari to download an image to your computer:

- **Internet Explorer.** Right-click the image, click Save Picture As, choose a location, edit the filename, and then click Save.

- **Firefox.** Right-click the image, click Save Image As, choose a location, edit the filename, and then click Save.

- **Safari.** Right-click (or Ctrl+click) the image, click Save Image As, choose a folder on your Mac, change the filename, and then click Save.

Once the image file is safely stowed on your machine, upload it to your Web site using either an FTP program or the upload tool provided by your Web host.

If your Web host provides an online editor, use it to insert your badge. How you do this varies depending on the host, but the basic steps are pretty much universal: Open the page in the editor, place the cursor where you want the image to appear, click the editor's image tool, and then choose the Twitter badge file. Click the image to select it, click the editor's link tool, and then specify the address http://twitter.com/*yourname*, where *yourname* is your Twitter username.

If you add stuff to your site by editing HTML, open the page or file in your HTML editor, place the cursor where you want the badge to appear, and then insert the image and link using the following HTML code:

```
<a href="http://twitter.com/yourname">
<img src="filename" />
</a>
```

Here, you need to replace *yourname* with your Twitter username and *filename* with the name of the badge file (for example, twitter.png).

If you uploaded the badge to a folder, then you need to alter the code slightly. For example, if the badge resides in a folder named graphics, change the code to this:

```
<a href="http://twitter.com/yourname">
<img src="/graphics/filename" />
</a>
```

By default, images are aligned on the left side of the page (or whatever page element — such as a table — they're sitting in). If you want the image aligned on the right, add the following code inside the `<img>` tag: `style="text-align: right"`.

Displaying a badge that shows your total followers

If you have a successful Twitter account that's amassed a sizable following, you might feel like bragging about it. I don't mean that you should cover the top of your page with a massive banner that shouts out your total followership. Please don't do that. I'm talking here about something a lot more subtle: a Twitter badge that not only points to your Twitter home page, but also includes a regularly updated count of your followers.

caution No matter how successful you are on Twitter, it's always considered bad Twitter etiquette to brag (or even mention) how many followers you have. Other successful tweeters won't care, less-successful tweeters might feel jealous, and I guarantee more than a few of your followers will abandon ship and stop following you.

The code wizards at TwitterCounter (whom you meet again in Chapter 9) offer just such a badge, and adding it to your Web site is a relatively straightforward matter of copying and pasting some code. First, use your Web browser to navigate to the following address, where *yourname* is your Twitter username:

```
http://twittercounter.com/pages/buttons/yourname
```

TwitterCounter displays a page that includes a few button styles, as shown in Figure 7.2. (The site also lets you design your own button.)

Near each button style you see a text box that includes some HTML code. Here's an example:

```
<script type="text/javascript" language="JavaScript"
src="http://twittercounter.com/embed/?username=wordspy& style=bird">
</script>
```

This code points to a script that resides on the TwitterCounter site, and that script contains the necessary instructions for contacting Twitter and grabbing your current follower count. This all happens behind the scenes, and fortunately you don't have to give any of it a second thought (or even a first thought, for that matter).

After you decide which style you prefer, click inside the text box that appears below that style. Your browser automatically selects all the text, so press Ctrl+C (or ⌘+C on a Mac) to copy it. Now open your online or local HTML editor, place the cursor where you want the badge to appear, and then press Ctrl+V (or ⌘+V on your Mac) to paste the code. If you're working on a local copy of your page, be sure to upload the revised file to your Web site.

TWITTERCOUNTER POWERED BY twitter | | Show |

Home   @wordspy   Featured - Xmas special   Dashboard   Widget   Buttons   Search   Top 100 Users   T

Twitter followers buttons for wordspy   [Tweet This!]

Twitter Username

| wordspy |

Text color

| ffffff | 🖉 |

Background color

| 111111 | 🖉 |

[Generate preview & code]

Preview:

| 2319   Followers |
twittercounter.com

Copy/paste the following code to your blog to display the button:

```
<script type="text/javascript" language="JavaScript" src="http://twittercounter.com/embed
/wordspy/ffffff/111111"></script>
```

Big Bird Button

```
<script
type="text/javascript"
language="JavaScript"
src="http://twittercounter.co
m/embed/?username=wordspy&
style-bird"></script>
```

The bird button has the added advantage of showing your full follower count and being more visible. More visible = more followers!

2,319
Followers on
Twitter.com for
@wordspy

7.2 TwitterCounter offers several styles of buttons, each of which links to your Twitter home and displays your total number of followers.

Adding a "Tweet This" link to your Web site

A great way to get the word out about your Web site or some content on your site is to get people to tweet about it. The problem is that it requires quite a few steps to construct a tweet about a site or page, as the following general procedure shows:

1. **Navigate to the page and copy the page address.**
2. **Switch to Twitter and paste the address in the update text box.**
3. **Return to the page and copy the page title.**
4. **Head back to Twitter and paste the title in the update text box.**
5. **Add your own text and then send the tweet.**

Whew! However, you can do your would-be tweeters a favor by helping them to condense Steps 1 to 4 into a single click of a link, which ought to make them more willing to tweet about your site.

I'm talking here about creating a "Tweet This" link (or perhaps "Tweet This Site" or "Tweet This Post" or whatever fits your situation), which you place strategically on your pages (for example, at the end of a blog post or article).

If you use an online editor provided by your Web host, place the cursor where you want the link to appear and add the link text (such as "Tweet This"). Select the text, click the editor's link tool, and then type the following general address:

```
http://twitter.com/home?status=Title (URL)"
```

Here, replace *Title* with the title of the page, post, article, or whatever, and replace *URL* with the address of the item. Here's an example:

```
http://twitter.com/home?status=Word Spy (http://wordspy.com)"
```

If you need to edit HTML to add the link, open the page or file in your HTML editor, place the cursor where you want the link to appear, and then type the link using the following HTML code:

```
<a href="http://twitter.com/home?status=Title (URL)">
Tweet This
</a>
```

Again, replace *Title* with the item title, and replace *URL* with the item address. Here's an example:

```
<a href="http://twitter.com/home?status=Word Spy (http://wordspy.com)">
Tweet about Word Spy
</a>
```

Figure 7.3 shows how this code creates a "Tweet about Word Spy" link on my site. If a tweeter clicks that link, the browser switches to Twitter, asks the user to sign in, if he isn't already, and then displays the specified text in the What's happening? box, as shown in Figure 7.4. Now all the tweeter has to do is add his or her own text and fire off the update.

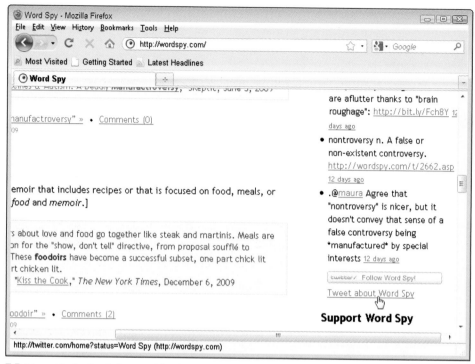

File Edit View History Bookmarks Tools Help

http://wordspy.com/

Google

Most Visited | Getting Started | Latest Headlines

Word Spy

nanufactroversy" » • Comments (0)
09

emoir that includes recipes or that is focused on food, meals, or
food and *memoir*.]

s about love and food go together like steak and martinis. Meals are
on for the "show, don't tell" directive, from proposal soufflé to
These **foodoirs** have become a successful subset, one part chick lit
rt chicken lit.
  "Kiss the Cook," *The New York Times*, December 6, 2009

oodoir" » • Comments (2)
09

are aflutter thanks to "brain
roughage": http://bit.ly/Fch8Y 1;
days ago

• nontroversy n. A false or
non-existent controversy.
http://wordspy.com/t/2662.asp
12 days ago

• .@maura Agree that
"nontroversy" is nicer, but it
doesn't convey that sense of a
false controversy being
manufactured by special
interests 12 days ago

twitter Follow Word Spy!

Tweet about Word Spy

Support Word Spy

http://twitter.com/home?status=Word Spy (http://wordspy.com)

7.3 A tweet invitation link on my Word Spy site

What's happening?   111

Word Spy (http://wordspy.com)|

Latest: Doug Coupland-"Brain research tells us that only 20 percent of human
beings have a sense of irony." For the 20%: http://frie... less than 5 seconds ago   update

7.4 Clicking the link in Figure 7.3 loads the link's status text into the user's
What's happening? text box.

TwitThis (http://twitthis.com/) is a service that offers custom "Tweet This" links and
even includes a built-in URL shortener that can save your potential tweeters another
step in the process.

Adding the Twitter Application to Your Facebook Profile

On the surface, Facebook, while ostensibly a member of the same social-networking club as Twitter, is a social horse of a different color. You can post photos and videos that people can comment on, you can write on a friend's wall, you can join groups, and you're free to encrust your profile with as many applications as you feel like configuring. However, although many Facebook users take advantage of all these social knickknacks, the truth is that all most Facebookers do is update their status every now and then.

As a nod to this reality, a while ago Facebook redesigned the user home page to display a "News Feed" of posts from friends and, most tellingly, a "What's on your mind?" text box at the top that you use to update your status, share information, or crack wise. Wait: a "What's on your mind?" text box? Remind you of anything? Of course! It's Twitter, Facebook style.

This leads to a very obvious question: If you're already using Twitter's "What's happening?" box to update your status, share information, or wisecrack, do you have to then repeat each tweet in Facebook's "What's on your mind?" box? You could, I suppose, post different updates in Facebook, but who has the time or energy to maintain two feeds? For that matter, who has the time or energy to post the same updates on two different sites?

Fortunately, you don't have to. The kindly coders at Twitter have come up with a Twitter application that you can add to your Facebook profile. This application includes an option to update your Facebook status when you post to Twitter, thus killing two social-network birds with a single tweet stone (or something).

The only downside to posting tweets to your Facebook profile is that Facebook doesn't convert @usernames to links and it doesn't use hashtags, so nontweeters might furrow their brows at these apparently nonsense references.

You can add the Twitter application directly via your Facebook account (click Applications, click Find More, and then run an application search for Twitter), or indirectly via Twitter. Here are the steps for the indirect method:

1. **Sign in to your Twitter account.**
2. **Direct your Web browser to http://twitter.com/badges.** The Get a Widget for Your Site page appears.

3. **Click the Facebook logo.**

4. **Click Continue.** The Add Twitter to Facebook page appears, as shown in Figure 7.5.

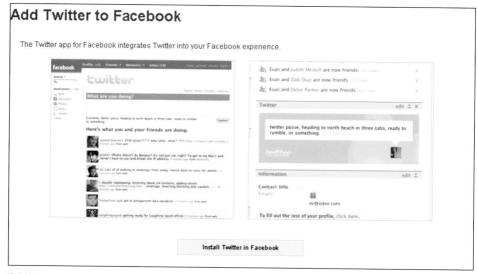

7.5 You can install Facebook's Twitter application from within Twitter itself.

5. **Click Install Twitter in Facebook.** If you're not already logged in to your Facebook account, Facebook prompts you to log in (or sign up, if you don't have an account). If you're already logged in to Facebook, the Allow Access page appears, so skip to Step 7.

6. **Type your Facebook account's e-mail address and password, and then click Login.** Facebook's Allow Access page appears.

7. **Click Allow.** Facebook asks you to log in to your Twitter account.

8. **Type your Twitter username and password, and then click Log in.**

note

If you see an error message after you click Log in, don't fret about it. Just click your browser's Back button and all will be well.

You end up at the Twitter on Facebook page, as shown in Figure 7.6. (To get to this page in the future, click Applications, click Edit, and then click Twitter.) The Twitter application shows your friend timeline as well as a What are you doing? text box, which you can use to post tweets from within Facebook. When you want to return to your real Twitter life, click one of the following tabs: Twitter Home, Profile, or Settings.

 For easier access to the Twitter application, click the Bookmark Twitter link at the bottom of the page to add the Twitter application to your list of Facebook bookmarks. If you don't see that link, click Applications, click Edit Applications, and then click the Edit Settings link beside the Twitter application. In the Edit Twitter Settings dialog box, display the Bookmark tab, select Bookmark Twitter, and then click Okay.

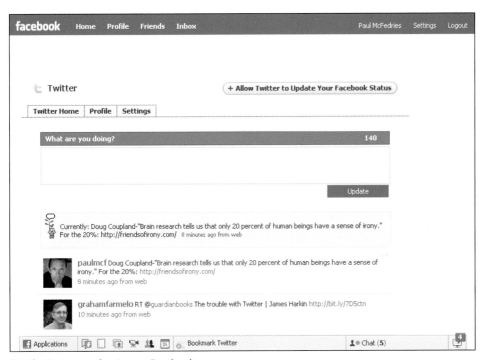

7.6 The Twitter application on Facebook

If you want your tweets to also get posted as your Facebook status updates, click Allow Twitter to Update Your Facebook Status. When the Twitter application asks you to confirm, click Allow Status Updates. (Note that this just means that your Twitter updates also get posted as Facebook status updates; if you post a status update on Facebook itself, that update is not sent to Twitter.)

To turn off automatic status updates from Twitter, click Applications, click Edit
Applications, and then click the Edit Settings link beside the Twitter application. In
the Edit Twitter Settings dialog box, display the Additional Permissions tab, deselect
Publish to Streams, and then click Okay.

Inserting the Twitter Flash Widget on Your MySpace Page

If you have a MySpace account, you can let your MySpace friends know that you have a secret
Twitter identity. Twitter offers a Flash-based widget that displays your recent Twitter updates.
Actually, there are two widgets to choose from (see Figure 7.7 a bit later in this chapter):

- **Interactive widget.** This widget shows your username, avatar, and the number of
  people who follow you. It contains a scrollable list of your last few tweets and also
  enables MySpacers to log in to their Twitter accounts and then interact with the widget
  by following you, replying to a tweet, or marking a tweet as a favorite. Tweet links also
  work, including @username links to Twitter profiles. This interaction is a great feature
  that will hopefully get lots of MySpace users to follow you.

- **Display-only widget.** This simple widget displays a shorter list of your recent tweets
  along with a link to your Twitter profile page. MySpace users can't interact with this
  widget, so it's less useful as a marketing tool for your Twitter account.

First, you need to get the widget code. Here are the steps to follow:

1. **Sign in to your Twitter account.**
2. **Navigate to http://twitter.com/badges.** You see the Get a Widget for Your Site page.
3. **Click the MySpace logo.**
4. **Click Continue.** The Which Flash widget page appears, as shown in Figure 7.7.

You need Adobe Flash Player to see the widgets, so if Internet Explorer displays the Information bar telling you that the site wants to run the Adobe Flash Player Installer, click the Information bar and then click Install This Add-on, and then click Yes when asked to confirm. If Firefox tells you that additional plug-ins are required, click Install Missing Plugins.

5. **Select the widget you want to install, and then click Continue.** You see either the Set up your Twitter widget page (if you selected the interactive widget; see Figure 7.8) or the Customize Your Widget page (if you selected the display-only widget).

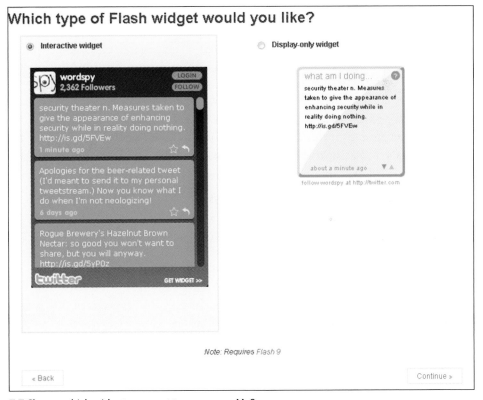

7.7 Choose which widget you want to grace your MySpace page.

6. **Customize your widget as follows:**

- **Interactive widget.** Use the Select a style list to choose a predefined design for the widget, and use the Widget size list to choose a width (narrow, wide, or full).

- **Display-only widget.** Click Badge Color and then click the color you prefer.

7. **Copy the code:**

- **Interactive widget.** Click the Copy link.

- **Display-only widget.** Click Copy to Clipboard.

7.8 Use this page to customize your widget.

With your code copied and ready for its MySpace debut, follow these steps to edit your MySpace profile:

1. **Log in to your MySpace account.**

2. **Click Edit Profile.** The Edit Profile page appears.

3. **Click inside the section where you want the widget to appear.** For example, you might want to use the About Me section or the General section.

4. **Press Ctrl+V (⌘+V on your Mac) to paste the code.** Figure 7.9 shows some code pasted into the About Me box.

5. **Click Save Changes.** MySpace displays a captcha for security.

6. **Type the letters you see in the image, and then click Save Changes.** MySpace adds the widget to your profile, as shown in Figure 7.10.

7.9 Paste the code into the section where you want the widget to appear on your MySpace page.

7.10 The interactive Twitter widget displayed on a MySpace page.

Displaying Your Twitter Updates on Your Blogger Site

If you've got a Blogger.com blog on the side, you might want to spice it up by displaying your latest tweets. You can do that by adding a Twitter widget to your blog sidebar. This widget shows your most recent tweets (the default is 5, but you can easily customize that), as well as a Follow Me link to your Twitter profile. Tweet links (regular links and @username links) also work, so your blog readers can check out the sites you include in your updates.

Here are the steps to follow to add a Twitter widget to your blog:

1. **Sign in to your Twitter account.**

2. **Point your Web browser at http://twitter.com/badges.** The Get a Widget for Your Site page appears.

3. **Click the Blogger logo.**

4. **Click Continue.** The Add Twitter to your Blogger blog page appears, as shown in Figure 7.11. The right side of the window shows a preview of the widget.

Add Twitter to your Blogger blog

Number of tweets: 5 ▼

Title: Twitter Updates

☐ No Title

Insert into your Blog

[⊕ Add to Blogger] If you're using new Blogger Layouts (or are not sure), just click the button on the left.

If you're not using new Blogger layouts, just grab the code and insert it into the sidebar of your blog template.

Preview

Twitter Updates

Doug Coupland-"Brain research tells us that only 20 percent of human beings have a sense of irony." For the 20%: http://friendsofirony.com/ 24 minutes ago

RT @allbeernews: Redhook Double Black Stout (with Coffee) http://ff.im/-djCjU [That has *got* to be good!] 5 days ago

I'm tickled amber that my favorite brewery has a Twitter feed. [RT @MillStreetBrew: @paulmcf what an insightful piece of beverage analysis.] 5 days ago

@MillStreetBrew Also, I believe your Organic Lager may well be the world's most thirst-quenchingest beer. 5 days ago

@MillStreetBrew Yes! I have spent many delightful hours in the company of your Tankhouse Ale. 5 days ago

follow me on Twitter

7.11 Use this page to customize your Twitter widget.

5. **Use the Number of tweets list to select the size of the tweet list.**

6. **Use the Title text box to change the title if you don't like the default Twitter Updates title.** If you don't want a title at all, select the No Title check box.

7. **Click Add to Blogger.** If you're signed in to your Blogger account, the Add Page Element page appears, so skip to Step 9; if you're not signed in, the Blogger: Sign In page appears.

8. **Type your Google account e-mail address and password, and then click Sign in.** The Add Page Element page appears.

9. **Use the Select a blog list to choose the blog you want to use, if you have more than one.**

10. **Once again you get a chance to edit the title by modifying the Title text.**

11. **If you want to adjust the widget code, click Edit Content to display the code, as shown in Figure 7.12.** I talk about this code a bit later in this chapter and give you a few suggestions for customizing it.

12. **Click Add Widget.** Blogger adds the Twitter widget to the Layout tab.

13. **Click Save.** Blogger saves the changes to your blog.

You can now click View Blog to see your blog with its shiny, new Twitter widget (Figure 7.13 shows an example).

Add Page Element

You're about to add content from another site to your blog. **Make sure you trust this site before proceeding.** This action will place some code from the content provider into your blog page. You can view the code details below.

Select a blog: Word Nooz ▼

Title: Twitter Updates

▼ Edit Content:

```
<div id="twitter_div">
<h2 style="display:none;" class="sidebar-title">Twitter
Updates</h2>
<ul id="twitter_update_list"></ul>
<a id="twitter-link" style="display:block;text-
align:right;" href="http://twitter.com/paulmcf">follow me
on Twitter</a>
</div>
<script src="http://twitter.com/javascripts/blogger.js"
```

▶ Edit Template:

ADD WIDGET   Learn more

7.12 Twitter copies the code for the widget to the Blogger's Add Page Element page.

📅 Tuesday, December 29, 2009

UN Establishes Vowel Relief Fund

AIEA, Hawaii—Former United Nations Secretary General Boutros-Boutros Ghali and current United Nations Undersecretary for Alphabet Mobilization Yada-Yada Yada announced today the formation of the United Nations International Vowel Assistance Committee. UNIVAC's mandate is "to help the vowel-deprived wherever they may live and to fund vowel relief efforts in the hardest hit areas."

"We have a good stockpile of a's, e's, and o's," said Ng Ng, UNIVAC's Letter Distribution Officer. "We hope to have an adequate supply of i's and u's over the next six months. In the meantime, we can use our extra y's in a pinch."

"Vowels of every description are badly needed," said Cwm Pffft, an activist with the group Consonant Watch. "The people in places such as Srpska Crnja and Hwlffordd are suffering horribly."

When asked to comment on the news, writer and animated film voice specialist Sarah Vowell said, "I haven't the faintest idea what you're talking about. Leave me alone."

 Posted by Paul at 2:09 PM 0 comments ✎

Twitter Updates

- Doug Coupland-"Brain research tells us that only 20 percent of human beings have a sense of irony." For the 20%: http://friendsofirony.com/ 37 minutes ago
- RT @allbeernews: Redhook Double Black Stout (with Coffee) http://ff.im /-diCiU [That has *got* to be good!] 5 days ago
- I'm tickled amber that my favorite brewery has a Twitter feed. [RT @MillStreetBrew: @paulmcf what an insightful piece of beverage analysis.] 5 days ago
- @MillStreetBrew Also, I believe your Organic Lager may well be the world's most thirst-quenchingest beer. 5 days ago
- @MillStreetBrew Yes! I have spent many delightful hours in the company of your Tankhouse Ale. 5 days ago
- Since I only drink liquids that contain caffeine or alcohol, it follows that Mill St. Brewery's Coffee Porter is my perfect drink #MyBeer 6 days ago
- Got the Bach cranked because the wind sounds like a wailing lunatic just outside my office window. At least I *think* it's the wind... 6 days ago

follow me on Twitter

7.13 A Blogger blog with a Twitter widget in the sidebar

Including Your Tweets on Your TypePad Blog

If you're a TypePad customer, you can let your blog visitors know about your Twitter shenanigans by adding a Twitter widget to your blog sidebar. Best of all, Twitter offers a widget that's not only configured for TypePad, but it will also add the widget for you automatically.

The automatic insertion feature should work with most TypePad blogs, but the exception is if your blog uses TypePad's advanced templates, which Twitter can't update automatically. I show you how to do it by hand a bit later.

Adding the Twitter widget automatically

Here are the steps to follow to add a Twitter widget to your TypePad blog:

1. **Sign in to your Twitter account.**

2. **Send your Web browser to http://twitter.com/badges to open the Get a Widget for Your Site page.**

3. **Click the TypePad logo.**

4. **Click Continue.** The Add Twitter to your TypePad weblog page appears, as shown in Figure 7.14, and you see a preview of the widget on the right side of the page.

5. **Use the Number of tweets list to select the size of the tweet list.**

6. **Use the Title text box to change the title to something other than the default (Twitter Updates).** If you'd prefer to go without a title, select the No Title check box.

7. **Click Install Widget on TypePad.** If you're signed in to your TypePad account, the Add a Sidebar Widget page appears, so skip to step 9; if you're not signed in, the TypePad login page appears.

8. **Type your TypePad account e-mail address (or username) and password, and then click Sign In.** The Add a Sidebar Widget page appears.

Add Twitter to your TypePad weblog

Number of tweets: 5 ▼

Title: Twitter Updates
☐ No Title

Insert into your Blog

[Install Widget on TypePad]

Note: This button won't work if your weblog utilizes Advanced Templates or Mixed Media Layouts. View the code to insert it yourself.

Preview

Twitter Updates

Doug Coupland-"Brain research tells us that only 20 percent of human beings have a sense of irony." For the 20%: http://friendsofirony.com/ 41 minutes ago

RT @allbeernews: Redhook Double Black Stout (with Coffee) http://ff.im/-djCjU [That has "got" to be good!] 5 days ago

I'm tickled amber that my favorite brewery has a Twitter feed. [RT @MillStreetBrew: @paulmcf what an insightful piece of beverage analysis.] 5 days ago

@MillStreetBrew Also, I believe your Organic Lager may well be the world's most thirst-quenchingest beer. 5 days ago

@MillStreetBrew Yes! I have spent many delightful hours in the company of your Tankhouse Ale. 5 days ago

follow me on Twitter

7.14 Use the Add Twitter to your TypePad weblog page to configure your Twitter widget.

9. **In the Configure section, select the check box beside each blog where you want the widget to appear.**

10. **Edit the title, if you feel like it.**

11. **Click Add Widget.** TypePad prompts you to change where the widget appears in your sidebar. By default, the widget appears at the bottom of the sidebar, so you might want to move it higher.

12. **If you want to configure where the widget appears, click Change Content Ordering, click and drag the Twitter widget to the new position, and then click Save Changes.**

You can now click View weblog to see your blog with its brand-new Twitter widget (Figure 7.15 shows an example).

News of the Word

Language news you won't find anywhere else (for good reason!)

Home   Archives   Profile   Subscribe

« UN Establishes Vowel Relief Fund | Main

• • • •

D E C E M B E R   2 9 ,   2 0 0 9

"Annoying" College Banished from Face of Earth

SAULT STE. MARIE, MICHIGAN—With only a few hundred unbanished words left in the language, the rest of the English-speaking world has voted to banish Lake Superior State University from the face of the earth.

The college, based in Sault Ste. Marie, Michigan, is famous for its annual Words Banished from the Queen's English for Mis-Use, Over-Use and General Uselessness. In recent years the college has taken some heat for banning words such as "you," "donut," and "supercalifragilisticexpialidocious."

"Lake Superior State has become a bit too, well, superior," said adjective historian Red Black.

The list, really just a silly publicity stunt, has proved to be irresistible to an unthinking media

TWITTER UPDATES

Doug Coupland-"Brain research tells us that only 20 percent of human beings have a sense of irony." For the 20%: http://friendsofirony.com/ 54 minutes ago

RT @allbeernews: Redhook Double Black Stout (with Coffee) http://ff.im/-djClU [That has *got* to be good!] 5 days ago

I'm tickled amber that my favorite brewery has a Twitter feed. [RT @MillStreetBrew, @paulmcf what an insightful piece of beverage analysis.] 5 days ago

@MillStreetBrew Also, I believe your Organic Lager may well be the world's most thirst-quenchingest beer. 5 days ago

@MillStreetBrew Yes! I have spent many delightful hours in the company of your Tankhouse Ale. 5 days ago

follow me on Twitter

7.15 A TypePad blog showing off a Twitter widget in the sidebar

Adding the Twitter widget by hand

If your TypePad blog uses an advanced template, Twitter won't be able to update your blog automatically. Not to worry, though, you can still do it by hand. Here's how:

1. **Sign in to your Twitter account.**

2. **Go to http://twitter.com/badges to open the Get a Widget for Your Site page.**

3. **Click the TypePad logo.**

4. **Click Continue to open the Add Twitter to your TypePad weblog page.**

5. **Use the Number of tweets list to select the size of the tweet list.**

6. **Use the Title text box to change the title to something other than the default (Twitter Updates).** If you prefer to go without a title, select the No Title check box.

7. **Click the View the code link.** Twitter displays the widget code in a text box.

8. **Highlight the code and press Ctrl+C (or ⌘+C on a Mac) to copy it.**

9. **Log in to your TypePad account.**

10. **Click the blog you want to use.**

11. **Click the Design tab.** TypePad displays a list of the advanced templates your blog uses.

12. **Click the Content link.** The Content page appears.

13. **In the Categories list, click All.**

14. In the Modules list, click Embed Your own HTML.

15. Click **Add this module.** The Custom HTML window appears.

16. Edit the Label text to provide a title for the updates (such as Twitter Updates).

17. Click inside the HTML text box.

18. Press Ctrl+V (or ⌘+V on your Mac) to paste the widget code.

19. Click OK. TypePad adds the new module to the sidebar.

20. Click **Save Changes.** TypePad saves the template and now shows your tweets to your blog visitors.

Adding a Twitter Widget to Your Site

If you don't have a Facebook or MySpace account, or a Blogger or TypePad blog, you can still give your site visitors the gift of your tweets. Twitter actually gives you a choice of not one, not two, but seven widgets that you can add:

- **Interactive Flash widget.** This Flash-based widget shows your username, avatar, and the number of people who follow you. It contains a scrollable list of your last few tweets, and also enables visitors to log in to their Twitter accounts and then interact with the widget by following you, replying to a tweet, or marking a tweet as a favorite. Tweet links also work, including @username links to Twitter profiles.

- **Display-only Flash widget.** This simpler Flash-based widget displays a shorter list of your recent tweets along with a link to your Twitter profile page. Your site visitors can't interact with this widget.

- **HTML widget.** This HTML-based widget shows your most recent tweets (the default is 5, but you can customize that) as text, as well as a Follow Me link to your Twitter profile. Tweet links (regular links and @username links) work, so your site readers can surf to the sites you recommend in your updates.

- **Profile widget.** This JavaScript-based widget shows your most recent tweets (the default is 4) as text, your avatar, your name, and a link to your Twitter profile. In each tweet, the links (regular links and @username links) are clickable.

- **Search widget.** This is a JavaScript-based widget that shows the results of a Twitter search.

- **Faves widget.** This JavaScript-based widget shows the tweets that you currently have in your Favorites list.

- **List widget.** This JavaScript-based widget shows the latest tweets from one of your Twitter lists.

There are quite a few widgets and plug-ins available for WordPress blogs. To see a complete list, check out the WordPress section of the Twitter Fan Wiki: http://twitter.pbworks.com/WordPress. Also, there are lots of Twitter widgets available for any Web site. Go to Widgetbox (www.widgetbox.com) and search on "twitter" to see the available widgets.

Which widget should you choose? Personally, you can't go wrong with either the interactive Flash widget or the Profile widget because they're geared toward people with Twitter accounts, so they're more likely to help you gain followers. If you're worried about many of your site visitors not having the Flash Player installed, then the HTML widget is the way to go. Use the Search, Faves, or List widgets if you want to display something other than your recent tweets.

According to Adobe, the makers of Flash, 99 percent of Internet-enabled desktops have Flash installed (source: www.adobe.com/products/player_census/flashplayer/). Seems awfully high to me, but you can at least be sure that most of your site visitors are likely to have Flash Player installed.

Adding Twitter's Flash widget to your site

To add one of the Flash widgets to your site, you first need to copy the widget code. Here's how it's done:

1. **Sign in to your Twitter account.**
2. **Surf to http://twitter.com/badges.** The Get a Widget for Your Site page appears.
3. **Click Other.**
4. **Click Continue.** The Which type of widget would you like? page appears.
5. **Select the Flash Widget option, and then click Continue.** The Which Flash Widget page appears.

You need Adobe Flash Player to see the widgets, so if Internet Explorer displays the Information bar telling you that the site wants to run the Adobe Flash Player Installer, click the Information bar, click Install This Add-on, and then click Yes when asked to confirm. If Firefox tells you that additional plug-ins are required, click Install Missing Plugins.

6. **Select the widget you want to install, and then click Continue.** You see either the Set up your Twitter widget page (if you selected the interactive widget) or the Customize Your Widget page (if you selected the display-only widget).

7. **Customize your widget as follows:**

    Interactive widget. Use the Select a style list to choose a predefined design for the widget, and use the Widget size list to choose a width (narrow, wide, or full).

    Display-only widget. Click Badge Color, and then click the color you prefer.

8. **Copy the code:**

    Interactive widget. Click the Copy link.

    Display-only widget. Click Copy to Clipboard.

If your Web host provides you with an online editor, use it to insert your widget code. How you do this varies depending on the host, but here are the generic steps: Open the page in the editor, place the cursor where you want the widget to appear, and then press Ctrl+V (or ⌘+V on your Mac).

If you edit your pages locally, open the page or file in your HTML editor, place the cursor where you want the widget to appear, and then press Ctrl+V (or ⌘+V on a Mac). Save your work, and then upload the revised file to your Web host.

Adding Twitter's HTML widget to your site

If you opted to add the HTML widget to your site, here are the steps to follow:

1. **Sign in to your Twitter account.**

2. **Surf to http://twitter.com/badges.** The Get a Widget for Your Site page appears.

3. **Click Other.**

4. **Click Continue.** The Which type of widget would you like? page appears.

5. **Select the HTML Widget option, and then click Continue.** The Customize and Get the Code page appears.

6. **Use the Number of tweets list to select the size of the tweet list.**

7. **Use the Title text box to change the title if you don't like the default Twitter Updates title.** If you don't want a title at all, select the No Title check box.

8. **Highlight the code in the text box and then press Ctrl+C (⌘+C on your Mac) to copy it.**

If your Web host has an online editor, use it to insert your widget code. How you do this depends on the host, but here's the basic idea: Open the page in the editor, place the cursor where you want the widget to appear, and then press Ctrl+V (or ⌘+V on your Mac).

If you craft your site locally, open the page or file in your HTML editor, place the cursor where you want the widget to appear, and then press Ctrl+V (or ⌘+V on a Mac). Save your work and then upload the file to your Web host.

To ensure that your page still loads successfully even if Twitter is in fail whale mode (or having some other problem), cut the part of the widget code that starts with the first `<script>` tag and ends with the last `</script>` tag, and paste it near the bottom of your page (ideally, just above the `</body>` tag).

If you want to customize the Twitter widget code, there's not a lot you can do, but you're not without options. First, here's the default code (prettied up a little to make it easier to read; *username* is replaced by your Twitter username):

```
<div id="twitter_div">
<h2 class="sidebar-title">Twitter Updates</h2>
<ul id="twitter_update_list"></ul>
<a href="http://twitter.com/username"
   id="twitter-link"
   style="display:block;text-align:right;">
follow me on Twitter
</a>
</div>
<script type="text/javascript" src="http://twitter.com/javascripts/blogger.
   js"></script>
<script type="text/javascript" src="http://twitter.com/statuses/user_timeline/
   username.json?callback=twitterCallback2&amp;count=5"></script>
</script>
```

Here are a few customization ideas to consider:

- To change the title, edit the text between the `<h2>` and `</h2>` tags on the following line:

```
<h2 class="sidebar-title">Twitter Updates</h2>
```

- To format the title, insert a style attribute in the `<h2>` tag and add one or more text-formatting properties. For example, the following code displays the title with blue, 20-point text:

```
<h2 class="sidebar-title" style="color:blue; font-size: 20pt">Twitter Updates</h2>
```

● To change the text for the link to your Twitter profile, edit the following line:

```
follow me on Twitter
```

● To adjust the number of tweets displayed, edit the count value in the second `<script>` tag.

To learn more about how to work with Cascading Style Sheets, please see the Wiley book *Beginning CSS: Cascading Style Sheets for Web Design, 2nd Edition* by Richard York (ISBN 978047009670).

Adding Twitter's Profile, Search, Faves, or list widget to your site

The widgets in the previous few sections are the original Twitter widgets. Not too long ago, Twitter released a set of new widgets ("version 2") that look as good as the Flash-based widgets, but that are based on solid JavaScript code and Cascading Style Sheets, so you don't have to worry about whether your users have the correct plug-in to handle the Flash widgets.

As I mentioned earlier, there are four of these newfangled widgets to choose from: Profile, Search, Faves, and List. In each case, you customize the widget using four tabs:

● **Settings.** You use this tab to set the basic widget configuration, such as the title, the caption (which acts as a kind of subtitle), as well as widget-specific settings, such as the query to use for the Search widget.

● **Preferences.** You use this tab to set options for the widget, such as the number of tweets to display, and whether the widget shows avatars, tweet timestamps, and hashtags.

● **Appearance.** You use this tab to set the colors for the widget's background, text, and links.

● **Dimensions.** You use this tab to set width and height for the widget.

Here are the steps to follow to insert one of these widgets:

1. **Sign in to your Twitter account.**

2. **Surf to http://twitter.com/goodies.** The Twitter Goodies page appears.

3. **Click Widgets.** The Select Your Widget page appears.

4. **Click My Website.** Twitter displays links and descriptions for the four widgets.

5. **Click the widget you want to add.** Twitter displays the Settings tab for the widget.

6. Fill in the field to configure the widget's settings. The fields you see vary depending on the widget, but in all cases you specify a Title and Caption. Figure 7.16 shows the Search widget with a Search Query defined.

7.16 The Settings tab for the Search widget.

7. Click Preferences and then configure the widget's options.

8. Click Appearance and then configure the widget's colors.

9. Click Dimensions and then configure the widget's width and height.

10. Click Finish & Grab Code. Twitter displays a text box with the code.

11. Highlight the code in the text box and then press Ctrl+C (⌘+C on your Mac) to copy it.

If your Web host has an online editor, use it to insert your widget code. How you do this depends on the host, but here's the basic idea: Open the page in the editor, place the cursor where you want the widget to appear, and then press Ctrl+V (or ⌘+V on your Mac).

If you craft your site locally, open the page or file in your HTML editor, place the cursor where you want the widget to appear, and then press Ctrl+V (or ⌘+V on a Mac). Save your work and then upload the file to your Web host.

How Can I Take Twitter to the Next Level?

1 2 3 4 5 6 7 8 9

Twitter has the endearing trait of being sneakily addictive. Many people sign up assuming they'll just follow a few friends and maybe fire off the occasional tweet when the mood strikes. Before long, however, those few friends have turned into a few dozen, and tweeting withdrawal sets in whenever they haven't updated in an hour. If you find yourself with an unshakeable Twitter habit, this chapter certainly won't help! I take you through a collection of Twitter power tools that enable you to squeeze every last ounce of Twitter goodness from your account.

Twittering on the Desktop: Twitter Clients

I've mentioned elsewhere in the book that the real essence of Twitter, its secret sauce, if you will, is immediacy: A friend's tweet comes in, you read it; a thought surfaces, you tweet it; an interesting tweeter pops up, you follow her; a topic interests you, you search for it. If you happen to be hanging out on the Twitter site, then all of these Twitter itches (Twitches!) can be scratched without delay. (As an added bonus, you don't even have to constantly reload your friend timeline to see if there's anything new; Twitter is kind enough to let you know automatically if there are new tweets waiting for you.)

The rub here, of course, is that few of us have the staggering amount of leisure time required to constantly monitor the comings and goings of tweets and tweeters on the Twitter site. We have memos to write, spreadsheets to build, empires (however small) to rule. We have, in short, day jobs that require us to focus on local tasks.

Fortunately, that doesn't mean you have to sacrifice the real-time Twitter experience. In fact, if anything it's an opportunity to enhance Twitter immediacy because you can install on your local PC a Twitter client application that constantly shows you the latest tweets from your friends, and enables you to send tweets (as well as replies and direct messages), follow people, search Twitter, and more, all from the comfy and familiar confines of your trusty computer.

Unfortunately, Twitter desktop clients are thin on the ground. Or, I should say, *good* Twitter desktop clients are thin on the ground. There are quite a few programs out there, but most of them are fairly pathetic, and some of those even charge you for the privilege! To my mind, there are only two really good Twitter clients for desktop use — TweetDeck and Seesmic Desktop — and I cover them in the next couple of sections.

Raising your Twitter game with TweetDeck

According to Twitter statistics site TwitStat (http://twitstat.com/), as I write this the most popular way that people interface with Twitter is via the Twitter site, although the percentage of users recently fell below 19 percent, and is dropping slowly but surely. That means that more than 80 percent of tweeters use some sort of client, and of those, by far the most popular is TweetDeck, with more than three times the number of users as the next most popular desktop client.

That popularity isn't surprising because TweetDeck is loaded with features, and it wraps those features in an easy-to-use, attractive interface. TweetDeck isn't a Twitter client, per se, but more of a social media client because it can also integrate with other services, including Facebook,

LinkedIn, and MySpace. The focus here is on Twitter, of course, so I'll just take you through TweetDeck's Twitter-related features.

Getting started with TweetDeck

TweetDeck is an AIR (Adobe Integrated Runtime) application, which means it can run on multiple operating systems. As I write this, TweetDeck runs on most versions of Windows 7 and Windows Vista (although not the Home Basic versions), Windows XP, and Mac OS X. There's a separate download for Linux. Head for the TweetDeck site (www.tweetdeck.com), and click the Download button. Note that the installer first adds the AIR runtime files to your system and then it installs TweetDeck.

If you have trouble getting AIR installed via the TweetDeck site, you might have better luck installing it directly from Adobe. Surf to www.adobe.com/products/air/ to download AIR from there.

When you run the program for the first time, it prompts you to add a Twitter account (as well as Facebook and MySpace accounts, if you have them). Click Add a Twitter Account, type your username and password, and then click Submit. TweetDeck next prompts you to register for a TweetDeck account. This is an account on the TweetDeck server, and it enables you to synchronize your TweetDeck data between two or more computers, which is pretty cool. (You can always sign up for an account later if you just want to get tweeting.)

When the dust clears, the TweetDeck window appears, as shown in Figure 8.1. As you can see, the TweetDeck window is divided into three main columns (a fourth column, called TweetDeck Recommends, can be safely ignored):

- **All Friends.** This is your friend timeline, and TweetDeck checks for new tweets once a minute.

- **Mentions.** This is your timeline of replies sent to you and tweets that include your username. TweetDeck updates this list every 1 minute and 21 seconds.

- **Direct Messages.** This is a list of the direct messages you've sent and received, and TweetDeck updates the list every 2 minutes and 42 seconds.

TweetDeck is great and all, but it has one less-than-great feature: It plays a chirp every time you have at least one new tweet on your friend timeline. This gets supremely annoying after about 2 minutes, but you can save your sanity by turning it off. Click the Settings icon (it's the wrench near the upper-right corner of the window), click the Notifications tab, click Advanced Options for Columns, and then deselect each of the Alert Sound check boxes.

8.1 TweetDeck shows your friends' tweets, and your mentions and directs, all in one place.

Working with tweets within TweetDeck is straightforward: Move your mouse over the avatar of the tweet you want to mess with, and TweetDeck displays four icons:

- **Reply.** Click to send a reply to the tweeter.

- **Retweet.** Click to retweet the update to your followers. To send an old-fashioned retweet, click Edit then Retweet; to send a new-fashioned retweet, click Retweet Now.

- **Direct Message.** Click to send a direct message to the user (assuming the two of you follow each other).

- **Other Actions.** Click to see a menu that contains two items, as shown in Figure 8.2:

    - **Tweet.** Click this item to see a list of tweet-related commands, such as Favorite and Email Tweet.

User. Click this item to see a list of user-related commands (see Figure 8.2), such as Follow, Unfollow, and View Profile. (In case you're wondering, the Search command runs a Twitter search on the tweeter's username and displays the results in a new column.)

When you're ready to post a tweet yourself, click the Compose Update icon (the leftmost icon in the top toolbar). TweetDeck displays a What's happening? text box, as shown in Figure 8.3. However, this isn't your father's What's happening? text box. Although there are buttons galore here, three are supremely useful to your average Twitterholic:

8.2 Hover the mouse over a user's avatar to see the tweet options, click Other Actions, and then click either Tweet or User to see a menu of commands.

From. If you have multiple accounts set up in TweetDeck, you see a button for each one in the From section. To send an update to multiple accounts, click the button for each account that you want to use (the text in an active button turns from gray to white).

> **note** To add more accounts to TweetDeck, either click the plus sign (+) in the From section, or click Settings and then click the Accounts tab. Click Add New Account and then click the account type you want to add.

8.3 TweetDeck's Compose Update feature is loaded with useful options.

- **Auto Shorten URLs.** If you leave this check box selected, when you paste a Web address into the What's happening? box, TweetDeck automatically shortens it for you. (To configure the URL-shortening service that TweetDeck uses, click Settings, click the Services tab, and then click an item in the Select the Service You Wish to Use to Shorten URLs list. See Chapter 9 to learn more about URL shortening.)

- **Upload a Photo.** Use this button to share a picture with your followers (I also describe image uploading tools in Chapter 9). Click Upload a Photo, and then choose the picture you want to share. TweetDeck uploads the image to the default service and inserts a link to the image in the tweet. (To configure the photo uploading service that TweetDeck uses, click Settings, click the Services tab, and then click an item in the Select the Service You Wish to Use to Upload Images to Twitter list.)

When you're ready to fire off the tweet, press Enter (or Return on your Mac keyboard).

So much for the TweetDeck basics. The next few sections take you through three of TweetDeck's most powerful features: window configuration, tweet filtering, and search monitoring.

Configuring the TweetDeck window

One of TweetDeck's greatest strengths is its seemingly endless number of window configuration options. You can add more columns, remove existing columns, move columns left or right, adjust the window size to show more or fewer columns, and even shrink the window down to a single column. Here are the basic techniques to use:

- **Adding a column.** Beside the Compose Update button, you see the Add Column button (the + icon). Click that button to open a window that enables you to add a column to any of your accounts. Click the Twitter logo and then use the list on the right to choose which Twitter account you want to use (if you have more than one, that is). Click Core to see the list of columns you can add to the TweetDeck window (see Figure 8.4): All Friends, Mentions, Direct Messages, New Followers, and Favorites. (You can also display the TweetDeck Recommends column, TwitScoop (displays hot Twitter topics as determined by the TwitScoop service; see Chapter 9), and two services that require accounts — 12Seconds and StockTwits). You can also click Groups/Lists to add one of your defined Twitter lists or create a TweetDeck Group (a TweetDeck feature that's now obsolete); finally, click Search to add a search column (described a little later in this chapter).

- **Removing a column.** If you don't use a particular column, you should remove it to reduce clutter in the TweetDeck window. Hover your mouse over the column you want to remove, click the X in the upper-right corner of the column, and then click Delete Column when TweetDeck asks you to confirm.

⊚ **Changing a column's position.** You can move a column's position within the TweetDeck window by clicking the left and right arrow buttons that appear in the toolbar below each column. For example, if you have more columns than can fit within the TweetDeck window, a horizontal scroll bar appears so you can scroll your columns. If you find yourself constantly scrolling to a column you use frequently, consider moving the column to the left so that it's back on-screen.

⊚ **Using Single column view.** If you have a second monitor, a great idea is to display the TweetDeck on that monitor so you can keep an eye on your columns. If you're stuck with a single monitor, one alternative is to shrink the TweetDeck window down to a single column, and then move the window to the side of your monitor so that it's out of the way of your regular work. To make this happen, click the Single column view icon (it's fourth from the right in the upper-right corner of the window).

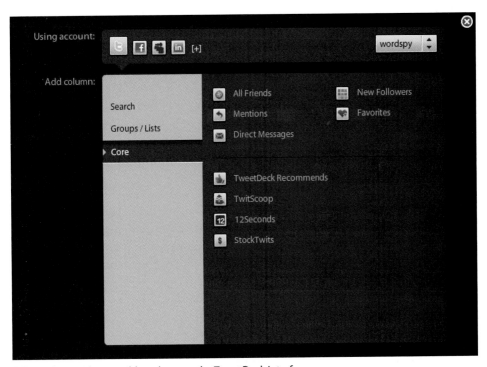

8.4 Use this window to add a column to the TweetDeck interface.

If you end up with more columns than can fit on your screen, you can configure TweetDeck to display narrower columns, which might improve things. Click the Settings icon (the wrench in the upper-right corner), select the Narrow columns check box in the General tab, and then click Save.

Filtering tweets

If you follow tons of people, then you're no doubt well aware that the tweets come in fast and furious, and keeping up is a full-time job that threatens to undermine your real full-time job. TweetDeck can help here by letting you filter a timeline to remove tweets that match some criteria, or to only shows tweets that match some criteria. Your criteria can be one or more of the following:

- **Text.** You specify a word or phrase and TweetDeck looks for matches within the text of each update.

- **Name.** You specify a word and TweetDeck looks for matches within the tweeter usernames.

- **Source.** You specify a word and TweetDeck looks for matches within the source of each tweet.

- **Time.** You specify a number and TweetDeck matches tweets that were posted within that number of hours.

The source refers to the client that the tweeter used to post the update. For example, updates sent via the Twitter site have the source web; not surprisingly, if a tweet was posted through TweetDeck, the source text is TweetDeck.

Here are the steps to follow to filter a column:

1. **Click the Filter this Column button.** This is the third button from the left in the column's toolbar (unless you're working with the leftmost column, in which case it's the second button from the left). TweetDeck displays the filter controls.

2. **Use the left list to choose the filter property you want to use: Text, Name, Source, or Time.**

3. **Use the second list to choose either Include (+) or Exclude (-).** If you choose Include, TweetDeck only displays those tweets that match your criteria; if you choose Exclude, TweetDeck does not display those tweets that match your criteria.

4. **Use the box to type your criteria text (or number, if you're creating a TimeFrame filter).** If you type multiple words, TweetDeck treats them as a phrase. TweetDeck immediately filters the column.

One of TweetDeck's most powerful and useful features is that it can analyze the content of a column and tell you the words, usernames, hashtags, and links that are the most popular. Click the Show What is Popular in This Column icon (the cloud) to display a cloud of the popular items, and then click the item you want to see. TweetDeck immediately sets up a filter to show just those tweets that include the item.

Monitoring a search

You saw in Chapter 6 that Twitter's search feature is a great way to get a feel for what Twitterers are currently saying about some topic. If you have a long-term interest in that topic, then you probably want to monitor the search results over time. Rather than rerunning the search periodically, I told you in Chapter 6 about a few services that can do the monitoring for you.

However, why bother with yet another Twitter tool when you can get the same result using TweetDeck? TweetDeck can create a column of tweets based on a Twitter search, and TweetDeck constantly monitors that search and displays the results in the column. Even better, you can create multiple search columns if you need to track multiple search queries. Nice!

Here are the steps required to create a search column in TweetDeck:

1. **Click the Add Column button in the toolbar (the + icon).** TweetDeck opens the Add Column window.

2. **Click the Twitter icon.** If you have multiple Twitter accounts, use the list on the right to select the account you want to associate with the search.

3. **Click the Search tab.** TweetDeck prompts you for your search string.

4. **Use the text box to type your search query.** The dialog box mentions that you can use OR and quotation marks, but actually any official Twitter search operator works here, as shown in Figure 8.5 (see Chapter 6 for the details).

5. **Click Search, or press Enter.** TweetDeck creates the new column and displays the search results, as shown in Figure 8.6. Note that you need to scroll the TweetDeck window to the right to see the new column.

8.5 Type a Twitter search string to define your TweetDeck search column.

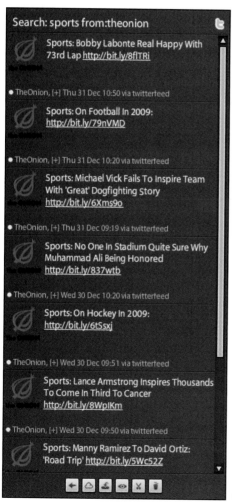

Controlling Twitter with Seesmic Desktop

After TweetDeck, the next most popular Twitter desktop client (at least as I write this) is Seesmic Desktop, and this popularity is well founded. Seesmic Desktop is a solid Twitter client that performs all the basic tweeting chores with ease. It can handle multiple Twitter accounts, offers a nice, multiple-column interface, and even throws in a couple of extra goodies to sweeten the pot.

8.6 The search column generated by the search query shown in Figure 8.5

Giving Seesmic Desktop a whirl

Seesmic Desktop is an AIR (Adobe Integrated Runtime) application, so it runs on multiple operating systems, including (as I write) Windows 2000, Windows XP, Windows Vista, Windows 7, and Mac OS X. Point your favorite Web browser at the Seesmic Desktop site (http://seesmic.com/seesmic_desktop/air/), and download the program. The installation program first installs the AIR runtime files (if your computer doesn't already have them), and then it installs Seesmic Desktop.

Seesmic, the company that makes Seesmic Desktop, also offers Seesmic for Windows (see http://seesmic.com/seesmic_desktop/windows/), which is a native Windows application (that is, it's not an AIR application). That should give Seesmic for Windows a clear edge in performance (because native applications almost always run faster than AIR applications), so it may be something to check out if you are a Windows user. Unfortunately, as I write this, Seesmic for Windows is so early in its development that it's nearly feature free. I hope that's changed by the time you read this.

Setting up your Twitter accounts

When you first launch Seesmic Desktop, you see the Accounts tab, which is where you manage your Twitter accounts. Here's how to get started:

1. **Type your Twitter username in the text box, and then click Add.** Seesmic Desktop adds the username to the Accounts list.

2. **Type your Twitter account password.**

3. **To add another account, click the plus sign (+).** Seesmic Desktop adds the username to the Accounts list.

4. **Repeat Steps 1 and 2 to type the account name and password.**

5. **Repeat Steps 3 and 4 to add other Twitter accounts, as needed.** Seesmic Desktop displays each account in a separate window.

6. **Click Save.**

Figure 8.7 shows a typical Seesmic Desktop window. The default view shows your friends timeline in the bulk of the window and an update text box, which Seesmic Desktop calls the input panel, at the bottom.

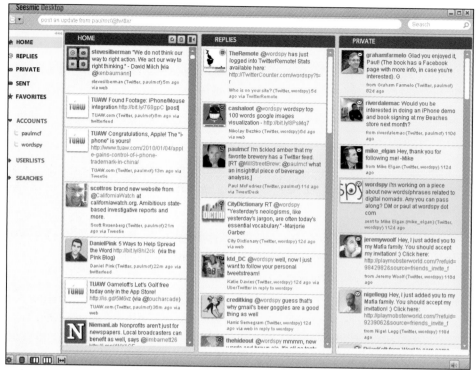

8.7 When you first open a Twitter account in Seesmic Desktop, you see a timeline of your friends' tweets (the Home column), mentions (the Replies column), and direct messages (the Private column).

To return to the Accounts tab after you've closed it, click the Settings button (it's the gear icon in the lower-left corner of the window), and then click Accounts.

Working with tweets

To work with a tweet, move your mouse over the avatar of the person who sent the tweet. As shown in Figure 8.7 (see the top tweet in the Home column), Seesmic Desktop displays four icons:

- **Reply.** This is the @ sign (top left) and you use it to send a reply to the tweeter.

- **Direct message.** This is the envelope icon (top right) and you use it to send a direct message to the user (as long as you follow each other, of course).

- **Retweet.** This is the chevron icon (bottom left) and you use it to retweet the message to your followership.

- **Actions.** This is the gear icon (bottom right) and clicking it displays a menu of actions you can take, including marking the tweet as a favorite, replying to all (that is, to the original tweeter as well as to anyone mentioned in the tweet), following and unfollowing the user, and more.

tip When new tweets come in, Seesmic Desktop beeps the speaker and displays a pop-up window briefly. If you have a couple of account windows open and a lot of incoming tweets, the incessant beeping and notifying is enough to drive even the most level-headed among us around the bend. To fix this, click the Settings button (the gear icon), click the Notifications tab, and then deselect the Enable Notifications check box.

Posting a tweet

As far as shipping out your own tweets goes, click inside the Post an Update text box at the top of the window and start typing at will. Seesmic Desktop has three extra doohickeys that you might find useful when constructing a tweet:

- **Share As.** If you have multiple accounts set up in Seesmic Desktop, click your avatar to the left of the text box to see a list of your accounts. Select the check box for each account you want to use for the tweet.

- **Add URL.** Click this icon to open the dialog box shown in Figure 8.8. Type (or paste) the address in the URL text box, select a site from the Service pop-up menu, and then click OK. (See Chapter 9 for more about URL shortening.)

8.8 Click the add URL icon to make a long Web address Twitter friendly.

- **Add Image.** Click this icon to share a photo with your followers using the photo-sharing service such as TwitPic (also described in Chapter 9). Choose the picture you want to share, and then click Post image. Seesmic Desktop uploads the image to the service and inserts a link to the image in the tweet.

When your tweet is sweet, click Send to ship it.

Navigating Seesmic Desktop

Seesmic Desktop's interface is a bit confusing at first, particularly if you have multiple accounts, because it lumps all your accounts together. For example, the Home timeline includes the tweets of all your accounts, and the Replies timeline includes the mentions for all your accounts. You might find this handy, but it's more likely that you prefer to keep your accounts separate. You can set this up by doing two things:

1. **Close the Home, Replies, and Private timelines by hovering the mouse pointer over each timeline and then clicking the Close button in the upper-right corner.**

2. **In the sidebar, click Accounts to display your accounts, and then click each account that you want to display.** Seesmic Desktop shows separate timelines for each account, as shown in Figure 8.9.

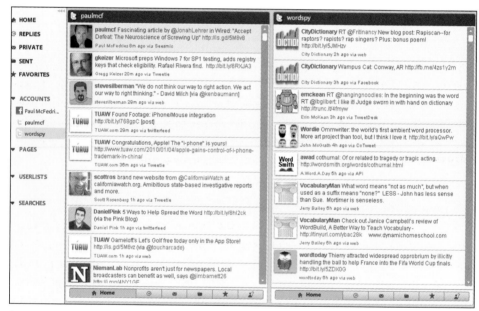

8.9 Close the default timelines and click an account to see just that account's tweets.

The simpler one-account-at-a-time layout shown in Figure 8.9 lets you focus on each aspect of your Twitter life. In each column, the friend timeline from your Twitter home page is the default view, but Seesmic Desktop actually has six panels in total, and you navigate among them by clicking the icons at the bottom of the window. Here's a summary:

- **Home.** Click this to see your friend timeline.
- **Replies.** Click this (it's the @ icon) to see your mentions.
- **Directs.** Click this (it's the envelope icon) to see the direct messages you've sent and received.
- **Archive.** Click this (it's the folder icon) to see the tweets you've sent.
- **Favorites.** Click this (it's the heart icon) to see the tweets you've marked as faves.
- **Lookup.** Click this (it's the person with a question mark icon) to look up a tweeter's profile. In the text box that appears, type the username and then press Enter or Return. Seesmic Desktop displays the user's profile data and his or her recent tweets.

Twittering on the Web: Twitter Web Sites

In the Anything You Can Do I Can Do Better Department, a number of Web sites have sprung up out of the ether in recent times to handle your tweeting chores, and their aim is to out-Twitter Twitter. They do that by offering useful features that tweeters crave, such as URL shortening, image sharing, and real-time updates. Toss in the advantage that you can use these sites to manipulate your Twitter world from any remote location where you have Web access, and Web site-based tweeting becomes a viable alternative to the desktop variety.

Seesmic Web

The Seesmic people don't seem to get much sleep, because not only do they have a couple of desktop clients (Seesmic Desktop, which I discussed in the previous section, and Seesmic for Windows), but they also maintain a pretty slick Twitter Web site at http://seesmic.com/app/. Head for the site, log in with your Twitter account, and then allow Seesmic access to your Twitter account. At first you only get Seesmic Web in preview mode. If you want to save your session and get other goodies you need to sign up for a Seesmic Web account.

Figure 8.10 shows the default Seesmic Web layout, which shows two columns, one for your friend timeline and one for your mentions. You use the sidebar on the left to add more columns for items such as messages you've sent, your favorites and direct messages, Twitter lists, and searches. (You use the Search box in the upper-right corner of the window to initiate a Twitter search.)

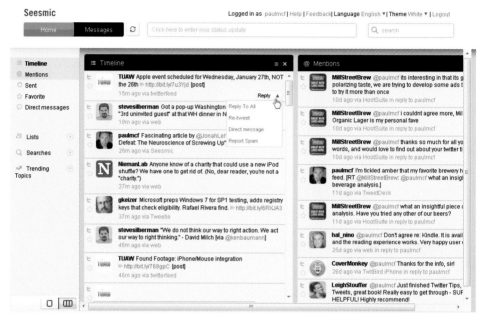

8.10 Seesmic Web is an excellent Twitter Web site.

Brizzly

One of the newest Twitter Web apps is Brizzly (http://brizzly.com/), which offers a nice, clean interface and lots of useful tweeting features. Once you add your Twitter account and authorize Brizzly to use your account info, you see the Home page, shown in Figure 8.11. You can use the timeline to reply to, retweet, and favorite each tweet, and you can navigate your other timelines by using the links on the left.

Brizzly is a solid Web app that has all the basic features you need, but it does offer one feature that I'd love to see incorporated into *every* Twitter client: a Mute button. It's an unfortunate fact of life on Twitter that some people simply post too often. Some folks are unrepentant overtweeters who always post dozens of messages a day, and there's not much you can do about that except unfollow that person. However, other tweeters who are perfectly reasonable most of the time may sometimes go on a tweet binge and post updates every minute or two for some reason. Unfollowing is too harsh a punishment for a temporary tweet barrage, so Brizzly lets you temporarily shut off that user's tweetstream. Locate a tweet from that person and click the username to see information and recent tweets from the person. However, as you can see in Figure 8.12, Brizzly also offers a Mute button. Click that button and then click OK to mute the user. This means that Brizzly doesn't show any tweets from that user in your timeline. Nice!

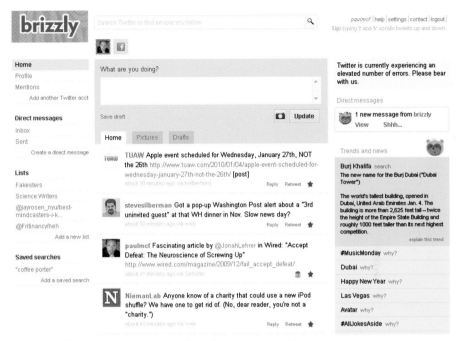

8.11 Brizzly offers a clean interface and all the features you could want.

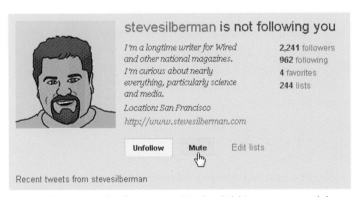

8.12 To silence a too-loud tweeter on Brizzly, click his username and then click Mute.

iTweet

iTweet (http://itweet.net/) is a full-featured Twitter interface with enough ebells and ewhistles to keep most Twitterers tweeting contentedly. After you log on with your Twitter username and password, you see the main iTweet interface, as shown in Figure 8.13. The page is divided into two vertical sections:

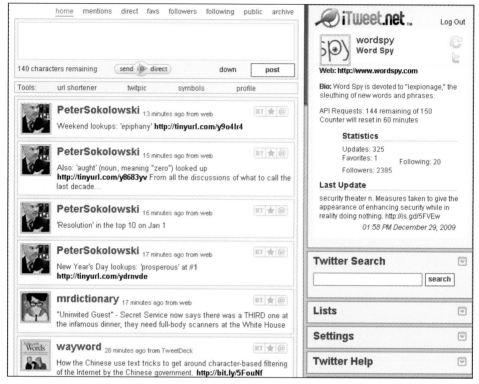

8.13 iTweet isn't much to look at, but it offers a full suite of Twitter-related features.

- The left column includes a posting area at the top and your friends' tweets below. The timeline is updated automatically (a feature that iTweet calls Autorefresh), so right off the bat iTweet is a step ahead of the Twitter site.

- The right column shows your profile info, your most recent tweet, and boxes for searching Twitter, configuring iTweet settings, and learning iTweet.

You work with the tweets by using the icons that appear on the right side of each update:

- **Retweet.** Click the RT icon to retweet the message to your followers.

- **Favorite.** Click the star icon to mark the tweet as a favorite.

- **Reply.** Click the @ icon to send a reply to the tweeter.

- **In reply to.** If the update is a reply, click this text to see the original tweet that the update is in reply to. This is a really nice feature, and it's often indispensable in letting you figure out what the heck someone's talking about.

To see a tweeter's profile data, click the person's avatar. To switch the display to a user's tweets, click the person's username (click Home at the top of the page to return to your regularly scheduled timeline).

When you get the urge to share, click inside the text box at the top of the page and type your missive. iTweet has three tweeting tools that you'll want to get to know:

- **URL shortener.** Click this tool, type a Web address in the Enter a URL to shorten text box, and then click Shorten. (See Chapter 9 for more about URL shortening.)

- **TwitPic.** Click this tool to share a photo with your followers using the TwitPic service (also described in Chapter 9). Type a description in the text box that appears, click Upload, and then choose the picture you want to share. iTweet uploads the image to TwitPic and posts the tweet.

- **Symbols.** Click this tool to display a collection of characters. If you see a symbol that would go well with your tweet text, copy the symbol and paste into your tweet.

If you want your tweet to be a direct message, click the Send direct button, type the username in the Direct Message to text box, and then click Send DM.

To check out iTweet's other sections, click the links at the top of the page:

- **Home.** Click to see your friend timeline.

- **Mentions.** Click to see the tweets that have mentioned you.

- **Direct.** Click to see the direct messages sent to you.

- **Favs.** Click to see the tweets you've marked as favorites.

- **Followers.** Click to see the people who follow you.

- **Following.** Click to see the users you follow.

- **Public.** Click to see what's happening in Twitter's public timeline.

- **Archive.** Click to see the tweets you've sent.

Tweetree

Tweetree (http://tweetree.com/) isn't a full-featured Twitter replacement, but that's okay because it offers a few features that you won't find anywhere else. To see what I mean, log in using your Twitter username and password to get to your Tweetree home page, as shown in Figure 8.14. You get the usual update text box at the top, followed by your friends' tweetstream. Each tweet has icons that enable you to reply, retweet, or mark the update as a favorite.

8.14 Your Tweetree home page shows your friends' tweets, but with a difference.

Here's where you notice the first of Tweetree's unique features (see the first tweet shown in Figure 8.14). If a tweet includes a shortened URL, Tweetree automatically ferrets out the original Web address and displays the page title (as a link) and the domain where the page resides. Why bother? Two reasons

- Many tweets introduce a shortened URL with only the barest-of-barebones descriptions: "Check this out doodz!!" or "This is funny LOL". Clicking the link more often than not wastes a few minutes of your precious time. By expanding the address automatically and showing the page title, you get a much better sense of what you're in for on the other side of the link.

- There's an inherent danger in a shortened URL because you simply don't know for sure where it will take you. Malicious users routinely use shortened URLs because they effectively hide the destination domain. With Tweetree, you not only see the domain, but you can hover your mouse over the link to see the full page address in the browser's status bar.

Either way, there's no more crossing of the fingers when you click a shortened URL.

I should mention, too, that Tweetree also looks for links to images on sites such as TwitPic and to videos on sites such as ffwd, and it automatically displays the media within the tweet, so you don't have to click yet another link to see yet another baby picture.

Finally, we come to the "tree" part of the Tweetree name. Tweetree examines your friends' tweets, and if it finds a reply, it grabs the original tweets and displays them using a (vaguely) treelike format, as shown in Figure 8.15. It's a nice way to listen in on a Twitter conversation.

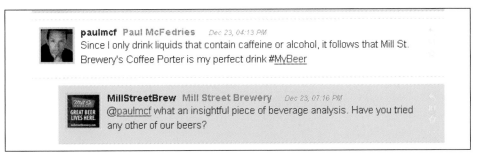

paulmcf Paul McFedries *Dec 23, 04:13 PM*
Since I only drink liquids that contain caffeine or alcohol, it follows that Mill St. Brewery's Coffee Porter is my perfect drink #MyBeer

MillStreetBrew Mill Street Brewery *Dec 23, 07:16 PM*
@paulmcf what an insightful piece of beverage analysis. Have you tried any other of our beers?

8.15 Tweetree shows replies and their original tweets in a treelike display.

Tweetvisor

Tweetvisor (http://tweetvisor.com/) is probably the most ambitious of the Web-based Twitter applications in that it doesn't compromise on features. Almost every bauble and bangle that you get on even the best desktop clients is available with Tweetvisor. The downside is that the interface is awfully busy, as you can see in Figure 8.16. (However, Tweetvisor does offer other themes that are less busy. Click Themes and then click the theme you want to use, such as Lite.)

8.16 Tweetvisor is a full-featured Twitter Web application.

Your Tweetvisor home page is chock full of stuff, so I'll just hit the highlights:

- **Mentions.** This is the left column and it shows the tweets that have mentioned you. Click and drag the Set refresh rate slider to specify how often you want Tweetvisor to check for new replies.

- **Tweet now box.** You use this box to send a tweet. It comes with a built-in URL shortener, and clicking the Tools link enables you to create tasks and shrink tweet text.

- **Tabs.** These are the buttons below the Tweet now box, and Tweetvisor offers 16 in all, including Friends/Lists, Me (your tweets), Favorites, Lists Manager (your Twitter lists), and Followers. Click Search to run a Twitter search that you can then save to the Saved Searches tab by clicking the Save this search link.

- **Hot Topic.** This section is designed to show you the results of a Twitter search. If there's a topic you're particularly interested in monitoring, run a search using the Search tab, and then click the Make topic HOT link. This displays the result in the Hot Topic section, where Tweetvisor will update the results automatically every few minutes.

- **Friends Timeline.** This middle column shows your friends' tweets. Click Refresh to see more, or select the Real-time check box to have Tweetvisor refresh the timeline automatically. Hover your mouse over a tweet to see icons for replying, retweeting, sending a direct message, and marking the tweet as a favorite.

- **DMs.** This column shows the direct messages that you've received.

Working with Twitter Gadgets and Widgets

If your desktop Twittering needs are fairly simple — you want to watch your friend's tweets go flying by, post an update every so often, and perhaps fire off the odd reply — then a big, fat desktop program or slow-to-load Web application isn't for you. Instead, you should consider a Twitter gadget or widget, a low-calorie application that lets you perform the basic Twitter tasks without getting in the way of your other activities.

Adding a Twitter gadget to your Windows Sidebar or Desktop

If you're running Windows Vista, you may have the Windows Sidebar tucked into the right side of your monitor. Sidebar displays gadgets, which are mini-applications dedicated to some small task, such as displaying the weather. There are a few Twitter gadgets out there for Windows, so if you want to use one of them on your PC, follow these steps to download one:

Gadgets are also available for Windows 7, although that version of Microsoft's flagship operating system has done away with the Sidebar and displays all gadgets right on the Desktop.

1. **If you're a Vista user, first make sure the Sidebar is displayed by choosing Start ⇨ All Programs ⇨ Accessories ⇨ Windows Sidebar.**

2. **Launch your favorite Web browser and use it to navigate to http://gallery.live.com/.** The Windows Live Gallery page appears.

3. **In the search box, type twitter and press Enter.** Windows Live Gallery displays all the gadgets that match your search term.

4. **Click the Sidebar gadgets link.** Windows Live Gallery displays all the Twitter gadgets, as shown in Figure 8.17.

5. **Check out the gadgets by clicking the link under each gadget thumbnail.** In the page that appears, you see a description of the gadget, user reviews, the number of downloads, and more. Use this information to select a gadget that suits you.

6. **Display the page for your gadget of choice and click Download.** Windows Live Gallery displays a warning that you should only install gadgets from developers you trust.

8.17 Windows Live Gallery offers quite a few Twitter gadgets.

7. **Click Install.** The File Download dialog box appears.

8. **Click Open.** The Internet Explorer Security dialog box appears.

9. **Click Allow.** The Windows Sidebar - Security Alert dialog box appears. Grrr!

10. **Click Install.** Finally, your gadget appears in the Sidebar (or on the Desktop in Windows 7).

11. **Configure your gadget with your Twitter credentials and whatever other options the gadget offers.** To configure a gadget, move the mouse pointer over the gadget, and then click the wrench icon (see Figure 8.18).

Adding a Twitter widget to your Mac Dashboard

If you want to do the Twitter thing using Mac's Dashboard application, there's a widget called (not even remotely surprising) Twidget that's worth the download. Here's how to get it:

8.18 A Twitter gadget alive and well on the Windows 7 Desktop

1. **Open Safari (or whatever Web browser you prefer) and direct it to www.apple.com/downloads/dashboard/.** The Dashboard Widgets page appears.

2. **In the Search box, type twidget.** The page displays a link to the Twidget widget.

3. **Click Twidget.** The download page for Twidget appears.

4. **Click Download.** Your browser downloads the widget and the Widget Installer appears.

5. **Click Install.** Within seconds, Dashboard opens and you see Twidget ready and raring to go.

6. **Type your Twitter username and password, and choose My Friends in the Timeline Display pop-up menu.**

7. **Click Done.**

8. **Click Keep.** Figure 8.19 shows the Twidget widget running in Dashboard.

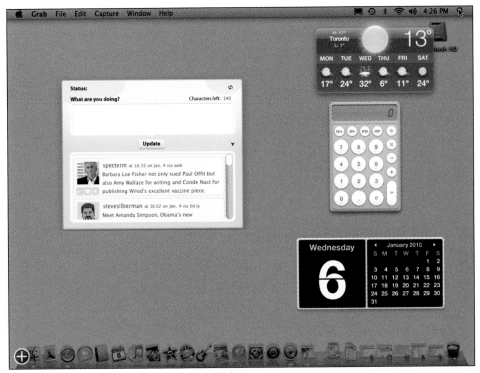

8.19 Twidget lets you post updates; monitor your friends' tweets; and replay, retweet, and favorite those tweets.

Adding a Twitter gadget to your iGoogle page

If you've got a customized iGoogle page loaded with gadgets, why not add a Twitter gadget into the mix? Here's how:

1. **Go to your iGoogle page by surfing to www.google.com/ig.**
2. **If you don't have an automatic sign-in, click Sign In, type your Google e-mail address and password, and then click Sign in.**
3. **Click the Add stuff link.** Google displays the Gadgets tab.
4. **In the Search for gadgets text box, type twitter and click Search.** Google displays a list of Twitter gadgets.

5. **Check out the gadgets by clicking the link for each gadget.** In the page that appears, you see a screen shot, a description of the gadget, user reviews, the number of downloads, and more. Use this information to select a gadget that suits you.

6. **Display the page for your preferred gadget and then click Add it now.** Google adds the gadget to your iGoogle home page.

7. **Click Back to iGoogle home.**

8. **Use the gadget to log in to your Twitter account.** Figure 8.20 shows TwitterGadget in my iGoogle home page.

8.20 You can tweet right from your iGoogle home page by adding a Twitter gadget.

Displaying tweets in Firefox

If you're a Firefox fan, you probably won't be surprised to know that you can customize the browser with Twitter-related extensions. These are mostly simple apps that show your friends' tweets and let you post updates. Here are the three most popular Twitter extensions for Firefox:

● **Echofon.** This extension (formerly called TwitterFox; it's available from http://echofon.com/) adds an Echofon icon in the bottom-left corner of the Firefox window. After installing, click the icon to type your Twitter account credentials. Echofon looks for new tweets every 5 minutes and then lets you know when new updates arrive. Click the Echofon icon to see the tweets or post one of your own (see Figure 8.21).

● **Power Twitter.** This extension (get it directly from the Mozilla Downloads page at https://addons.mozilla.org/en-US/firefox/addon/9591) is actually designed to enhance the Twitter.com site. Power Twitter adds new features to Twitter such as converting shortened URLs to their original addresses, showing images and videos within the tweet (see Figure 8.22), adding buttons to share a photo and shorten a URL to the update box, adding a Search box in your sidebar, adding a retweet icon to each update, and integrating Twitter with Facebook.

8.21 Click the Echofon icon to see your incoming friend feed or post a tweet.

What's happening?   140

| Post Photo | Shorten Link | Your Mood? | Today's Question! |

Latest: Fascinating article by @JonahLehrer in Wired: "Accept Defeat: The
Neuroscience of Screwing Up" http://is.gd/5M8v8 about 3 hours ago   update

Home

stevesilberman [via @kwestin] The iSlate revealed:

14 minutes ago from web

carlzimmer Loom: This fall, I gave a number of lectures about the
evolution of swine flu. By the time I got to the end of the ...

Evolving Viruses To Death | The Loom | Discover Magazine

8.22 Power Twitter extends Twitter.com by adding inline images,
deshortening shortened URLs, and more.

Some of Power Twitter's features only come alive if you give the extension your
Twitter password. To do that, click the Settings link that appears in the lower-right
corner of the screen.

- **TwitKit.** This extension (get it here: https://addons.mozilla.org/en-US/firefox/addon/6845)
  adds a sidebar to Firefox, as you can see in Figure 8.23. It's a pretty standard Twitter
  client that enables you to post updates, see your friends' tweets (updated automatically;
  yes!); reply and favorite those tweets; and view lists of your friends, followers, replies, and
  tweets.

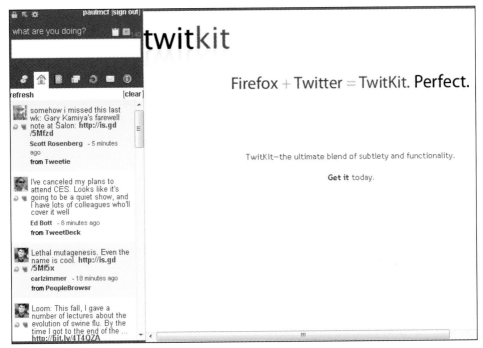

8.23 TwitKit is a Firefox sidebar extension that lets you work with your Twitter account.

What Tools Can I Use to Extend Twitter?

1 2 3 4 5 6 7 8 **9**

At its heart, Twitter is based on a refreshingly simple premise: You post short updates about what's happening in your life, follow your friends' updates, and create conversations around those updates. So it's more than a little odd that such a simple service would end up with this massive ecosystem of applications, Web sites, utilities, and other tools that aim to extend and enhance the basic Twitter experience. But the other idea at the heart of Twitter is openness, and making most profiles and tweets available to all comers has enabled the world's programming geniuses to come up with some eye-poppingly useful tools, as you see in this chapter.

Shortening URLs

Typing a tweet and watching the ubiquitous characters-you-have-left counter fall is like being in one of those movie scenarios where the walls of a room slowly close in on the hero. The closer you get to zero, the more tense you feel, and the more pressure there is to escape before it's too late!

One of the more common Twitter conundrums occurs when you write an admirably concise-but-coherent tweet, see that you've still got 25 or so characters to spare, breathe a sigh of relief, and then realize you still have to include a 75-character Web address. Doh! The solution is to knock that address down to size using a URL-shortening service. This is a Web site (usually; there are programs and plug-ins available, too) that accepts any Web address, no matter how long, and reduces it to a much shorter URL that's almost always less than two dozen characters (and often under 20).

For example, consider the following address (this book's Amazon.com page, actually):

```
http://www.amazon.com/Twitter-Tips-Tricks-Tweets-McFedries/dp/0470624661/
```

This is a 73-character address, which isn't super-long by modern Web standards, but it would still use up over half your tweet allotment. When I ran this address through the URL-shortening machine at bit.ly (http://bit.ly/), I ended up with this:

```
http://bit.ly/7r9UoP
```

The bit.ly service (like all URL shorteners) generates a random string of letters and numbers (usually five characters, but sometimes as few as four), and associates the resulting short address with the original address. When someone surfs to the shortened URL, bit.ly (or whatever) looks up the associated original URL and then redirects the Web browser to that address. Best of all, because the shortened address consists of (in this case) a mere 20 characters, you've just awarded yourself an extra 53 characters to (in this case) praise the book!

The clash between the immovable object of Twitter's 140-character limit and the irresistible force of people tweeting links to interesting and fun Web sites has created a boom in the URL-shortening business. Hundreds of services have sprung up, seemingly overnight, and it's now quite the cottage industry. That's great, but how on earth are you supposed to choose which service to use?

In some cases the answer is you don't have to. Many third-party Twitter tools come with built-in connections to URL shorteners, so you just type your address, click Shorten (or whatever), and away you go. Some, like TweetDeck and Seesmic Desktop, actually offer multiple shortening services, which narrows things down but still forces you to make a choice. If you don't like any of the services offered, or if you use the Twitter Web site to post and don't have direct access to URL shortening, then you must find your own.

note The Twitter Web site doesn't have a URL-shortening feature on its interface, but it does shorten URLs. If you post a tweet that includes a regular Web address, Twitter often shortens that address using the bit.ly service (http://bit.ly/).

To help you decide, here are a few things to look for in a URL-shortening service:

- **Short domain name.** This is probably the most important and the most obvious trait to look for. Clearly a service named, say, getyoururlshortenedheredude.com just isn't going to help all that much. The best sites have truly tiny domain names, from tinyurl.com (ironically, one of the longer names in this field) to is.gd (a four-character domain name such as this is the shortest-possible name).

- **Custom short code.** The four- and five-character codes generated by URL-shortening services aren't particularly memorable or informative. One of the signs of a good shortener is that it gives you the option to specify your own code. For example, if you want to share a link to your cubic zirconia jewelry auction on eBay, you could use, say, TinyURL to create a short address that's easy to remember (for example, http://tinyurl.com/cubicz) or informative (for example, http://tinyurl.com/CubicZirconiaAuction).

- **Link preview.** Many people are paranoid about shortened URLs because they give no indication of what lurks on the business end of the link. Hackers who have gone over to the dark side of the force often use short URLs to lure the unsuspecting into malicious sites. Less darkly, the site could be one known for excessive pop-ups, overuse of Flash and other media, or other annoying features. A good URL-shortening service will offer some way for users to preview the original address before actually going there. For example, is.gd (http://is.gd/) lets you preview a link by adding a hyphen (-) after the shortened URL.

- **Statistics.** How do you know if people are clicking your tweet links like crazy or ignoring them with a vengeance? The truth is, you don't. You may be able to tease some numbers out of your Web server log if you're linking to your own site (which just sounds like way too much work), and you're completely in the dark when it comes to links to other sites. Many URL-shortening services offer link statistics (they often call them *analytics*) that tell you (at the very least) how many times your short URL has been used. Stat geeks love sites such as cli.gs (http://cli.gs/) that offer reams of numbers: total hits, hits by day, hits by country, and more.

With all that in mind, here are a half-dozen URL-shortening services to consider:

- **bit.ly (http://bit.ly/).** This service is becoming very popular, mostly thanks to its short domain name and its setting as the default shortening service in Twitter and TweetDeck. It offers custom short codes, and if you sign up for a free account, you get stats that show total clicks, clicks by country, date, and more (see Figure 9.1). You can also post a tweet right from the bit.ly site!

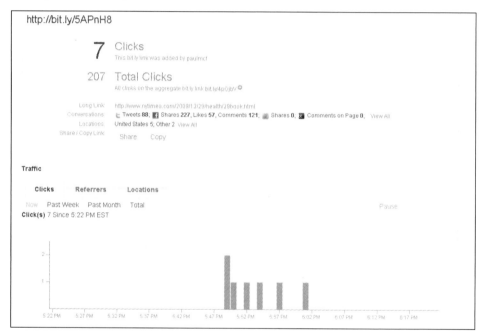

9.1 With a bit.ly account, you can track your link stats.

- **is.gd (http://is.gd/).** This service (it's pronounced "is good") is gaining ground in the URL-shortening race mostly because it uses a five-character domain and its short codes are only four characters, so a total is.gd short URL grabs just 17 characters of precious tweet real estate. You give users a link preview by adding a hyphen (-) to the end of the short URL, so adding the feature takes up only a single extra character. is.gd doesn't offer custom codes or statistics as I write this.

- **r.im (http://r.im).** I like this service because it's simple and its domain is maximally short, not to mention the short codes are just four characters. If you create a r.im account using the same username and password as your Twitter account, you can shorten a URL and post it to Twitter all at once.

Other minimalist URL shorteners to check out are 3.ly, a.gd, j.mp, l.pr, u.nu, x.vu, and z.pe.

- **TinyURL (http://tinyurl.com/).** This is one of the oldest and best-known services, and it's still one of the most popular, mostly thanks to its former position as Twitter's default URL-shortening service. It offers custom short codes and a link preview option (using the domain preview.tinyurl.com).

- **twurl.nl (http://twurl.nl/).** This is the service used by Tweetburner (http://tweetburner.com/), which offers extensive link statistics when you sign up for a Feedburner account. No custom short codes, however, and no preview feature.

- **cli.gs (http://cli.gs/).** This service has most of the basics, including a short domain and custom short codes. However, its forte is data, lots and lots of data. You can track not only hits, but hits by country and by social network, and you can even create separate URLs for different services (for example, one for Twitter and one for Facebook).

Having trouble shoehorning your text into a tweet? Then consider using the TweetShrink service (http://tweetshrink.com/), which trims text by converting certain words to short forms. (Note, however, that this site doesn't seem to work very well with Internet Explorer. Use Firefox or Safari instead.)

Sharing Photos, Videos, and Music

Facebook users get to share photos and videos with their friends, and MySpace users also get to share their favorite MySpace bands with their peeps. Twitter is, obviously, a text-only medium, so sharing media with your tweeps is out, right? True, you can't embed media directly into a tweet, but you can embed links to any media that you've added to other sites, such as Flickr and YouTube.

That works, but the entire process is a bit on the exhausting side, particularly if you want to share lots of stuff:

1. **Go to the site where your media is hosted.**
2. **Upload the media to the site.**

3. **Copy the address of the page that displays the media.**

4. **Go to a URL-shortening service and shorten the address from Step 3.**

5. **Go to Twitter or load your favorite Twitter application.**

6. **Compose a tweet about the media, paste the shortened URL, and then fire away.**

My, but that's an awfully roundabout way to perform a task that takes only a few mouse clicks on Facebook or MySpace. Ah, but the Twitterverse can be remarkably resourceful when it senses something missing from its vast toolbox. So now there are special Twitter-friendly sites where you can perform all of these steps in one place. It's the civilized way to share photos, videos, and music. The next few sections tell you about a few of these sites.

Sharing photos

If a picture is worth a thousand words, then a single photo is the equivalent of about seven tweets! Fortunately, you only have to post a single tweet to share a photo using any of the many photo-sharing services that support Twitter. In the next section, I show you how to use TwitPic and later I give you some info about a few other photo-sharing sites.

How nice would it be to view photos within your tweets rather than having to click to another site? Really nice! As I mentioned earlier, you can't embed media in a tweet, but an application can take an address that points to a photo, grab the photo, and then display the image along with the tweet text. Happily, we're starting to see this feature — usually called inline photos — added to more Twitter applications. For example, the iPhone app Twittelator Pro (see Chapter 5) displays inline photos, as do the Web sites Tweetree and the Firefox plug-in Power Twitter (both described in Chapter 8).

Using TwitPic

The gold standard in photo sharing for Twitter is TwitPic (http://twitpic.com/), which is by far the most popular photo-sharing service for tweeters. This is partly because almost every Twitter application that comes with some sort of "Share a photo" feature uses TwitPic to handle the dirty work of uploading the photo and shortening the URL. However, the TwitPic site itself is really easy to use, and you can even use TwitPic to upload photos by e-mail (from your camera phone, for example).

Here's the procedure to follow to upload a photo and post a tweet using the TwitPic site:

1. **Navigate to http://twitpic.com/ and type your Twitter account username and password.** Your TwitPic home page appears. The photos you post will appear here.

2. **Click Upload photo.** The Upload and post a photo page appears.

3. **Click Browse.** (If you're using a Mac, click Choose File.) The Choose File to Upload dialog box appears.

4. **Choose the photo you want to upload and then click Open (or click Choose on your Mac).**

5. **Type a message to go along with your photo, as shown in Figure 9.2.**

9.2 With TwitPic, you choose a photo, write a message, and then ship the tweet.

6. **Click upload.** TwitPic uploads the photo, shortens the photo's URL, and then posts that address and your message as a tweet (see Figure 9.3).

9.3 TwitPic takes care of shortening the photo URL and posting the URL and your message to your Twitter account.

note TwitPic also lets you tweet a photo from your mobile phone. In your TwitPic page, click Settings to see your special TwitPic address, which takes the form *username.pin*@twitpic.com, where *username* is your Twitter screen name, and *pin* is a four-digit number (which you can change). E-mail a photo to that address from your phone (your subject line is the tweet text), and it appears as a tweet a few minutes later.

Other photo-sharing services

TwitPic may be the Big Kahuna of Twitter photo-sharing services, but it's not the only game in that particular town. Here are a few others to check out:

- **Mobypicture (http://mobypicture.com/).** This service lets you share photos not only with Twitter, but with a wide variety of sites, including Facebook, Flickr, Jaiku, and blogging platforms such as WordPress and Blogger. For these other sites you have to create a Mobypicture account, but for Twitter, you don't need to create a new account (unless you want to, of course); instead, you log in using your Twitter credentials. You can then upload your photos using the Web site, via e-mail, MMS (multimedia messaging service), or the Mobypicture iPhone app.

- **Pikchur (http://pikchur.com/).** This site also supports a wide variety of sites, including Facebook, FriendFeed, identi.ca, tumblr, and many more. On the login page, be sure to choose Twitter from the list, and then type your Twitter account credentials. Once you're in, you can upload via the Web site or set up an e-mail address to post from your phone using e-mail or MMS.

- **SnapTweet (http://snaptweet.com/).** If you have a Flickr (www.flickr.com) account, you can use SnapTweet to post tweets that link to your Flickr photos. Sign in to SnapTweet using your Twitter account username and password, along with your Flickr address. You'll see your latest Flickr photo, and you can start uploading.

- **TweetPhoto (http://tweetphoto.com/).** This is a very simple photo-sharing site (hence the site's tag line, "Photosharing made simple"). After you log in with your Twitter account credentials, you browse for the picture file you want to use, compose a pithy message, and then ship it. It doesn't get any simpler than that! Click Settings to see your personal mobile e-mail address, which you can use to upload photos via TweetPhoto when you're on the move.

- **yfrog (http://yfrog.com/).** This site presents a simple interface (see Figure 9.4) that lets you upload either a local photo or a photo on the Web. Log in to your Twitter account, select an image (from a local file, a Web address, or your computer's Webcam), write an accompanying tweet (100 characters max), and then click Post It! to send the tweet. One of the nice features of yfrog is that when people click the link to load your photo, the yfrog page includes a ReTweet link that enables tweeters to easily retweet your photo. The yfrog site is also optimized for the iPhone, and pointing mobile Safari to yfrog.com displays the interface shown in Figure 9.5.

9.4 The yfrog site lets you upload local or Web-based images and post a link as a tweet.

Sharing videos

Although photo sharing is the type of media most often shared by tweeters, video is right up there, as well. That's not surprising given the immense popularity of YouTube and other video-sharing sites. Here are three Web sites that make it easy to share video with your Twitter tribe:

- **TweeTube (http://tweetube.com/).** This site is designed to help you easily share YouTube videos with your Twitter posse. The home page includes a text box that you use to paste the address of the YouTube video you want to feature (you can also use the TweeTube site to search for YouTube videos). Click Get Video and TweeTube retrieves the video, as shown in Figure 9.6. Type a message, type your Twitter account username and password, and then click share this video.

9.5 The yfrog site is iPhone-friendly.

- **Twiddeo (http://twiddeo.com/).** This new service lets you upload and share your own video with your tweeps. You can upload a video file from your computer, beam in a video captured on your phone, or even record a video straight from your Webcam.

- **TwitWall (http://twitwall.com/).** This site enables you to share not only videos, but also images and music files. Log in with your Twitter account credentials, click Add an Entry, and then specify a message and your video specifics. For the latter, click the Embed Tags tab and then your video code (such as the `<object>` tag code associated with a YouTube video).

9.6 TweeTube makes it easy to share YouTube videos with your Twitter pals.

Want to sample the videos that tweeters around the world are sharing with their friends? You could search Twitter for "video," and wade through all the nonvideo results, or you can take a trip to Twitmatic (http://twitmatic.com/), which dips into the stream of public timeline videos and lets you see what's being shared. Prepare to waste lots of time on this site!

Sharing music

Got a favorite song you want to share? That's awfully nice of you. Fortunately, sharing a tune on Twitter is easy if you use any of the following music-sharing sites:

- **Blip.fm (http://blip.fm/).** This site lets you set up your own broadcast station. Create an account and then configure it to share with Twitter by typing your Twitter credentials.

Locate a song from the Blip.FM archives, click Blip, type some text to appear in your tweet, and then click OK.

- **Song.ly (http://song.ly/).** This site is a combination music-search service and music-sharing service. Type an artist or song title and click Search, and Song.ly looks for matching music on the Web. In the results (see Figure 9.7), if you see the song you want to share, click the Tweet icon, sign in to your Twitter account, and then post the tweet.

- **Twiturm (http:/twiturm.com/).** You can use this site to share your own music by uploading an MP3 file, or to share Web-based MP3s by specifying a song's Web address. Log in with your Twitter username and password, and then click Upload. Specify a local file or a Web address, type a message for the tweet, and then click Upload.

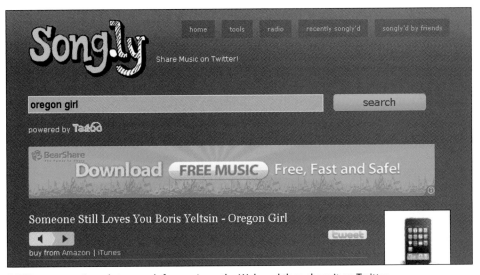

9.7 You can use Song.ly to search for music on the Web and then share it on Twitter.

- **twt.fm (http:// twt.fm/).** This site is by far the most popular music-sharing service among Twitter users. Twt.fm scours the Web for music, but it can also locate music streams on the Web or share your MP3 links. The home page asks for your Twitter username, an artist name, and a track name. Click Preview and, if twt.fm finds the track (see Figure 9.8), click Yes, Create It to switch to Twitter where you can post the tweet.

If your friends only share music occasionally, you can wait quite a while between music tweets, or you could miss a music tweet. Fortunately, you can use Twisten.fm (http://twisten.fm/) to cull just the music tweets from your friend timeline. Log in using your Twitter username and password, and Twisten.FM displays a Following list that displays the music shared recently by your friends. Click the Everyone list to see music being shared on the public timeline.

9.8 Use the twt.fm site to share music with your Twitter sidekicks.

Posting to Multiple Social Networks

It's becoming increasingly rare these days to find anyone who can make do with just a single social network. Most of us have two or three or more groups of online friends that we pester with status updates, but logging in to each site and firing off a separate message for each service just gets too time consuming. Fortunately, the world's programmers must also be social butterflies because they've come up with a few useful solutions that let you post a status update (and sometimes a photo or video, too) to multiple social networks.

Here are a few examples:

- **HelloTxt** (http://hellotxt.com/)
- **AIM Lifestream** (http://lifestream.aim.com/)
- **Twitterfeed** (http://twitterfeed.com/)

However, the most popular service among the overnetworked set right now is Ping.fm, which currently supports 46 social networks and seems to add new ones on a scarily regular basis. (I don't know about you, but I didn't even know there were 46 social networks until I joined Ping.fm!) These networks include all the major online hangouts, including Facebook, MySpace, Friendster, del.icio.us, Flickr, Jaiku, and, of course, Twitter.

That's impressive enough, but Ping.fm also raises eyebrows with its incredible variety of posting options: e-mail, mobile phone, SMS, MMS, instant messaging (AIM, Yahoo! Messenger, Google Talk, and Windows Live Messenger), gadgets (such as Ping.fm for iGoogle), Web applications (such as Twitterfeed (http://twitterfeed.com/) and the Ping.fm application on Facebook), and desktop applications (such as twhirl).

Getting started with Ping.fm

Your first chore is to sign up, which you can do by following these steps:

1. **Make a beeline with your browser for http://ping.fm/.**

2. **Click Signup.**

3. **Type your e-mail address and a password (twice).**

4. **Click Signup.** Ping.fm creates your account and displays the Manage Social Networks page, as shown in Figure 9.9.

P > Manage Social Networks		Edit Profile	Settings	Recent Posts	My Media	Help

Below is a list of social networks you have yet to hook in to your Ping.fm account. Setup is easy. Just click the "Add Network" and follow the directions on the service page.

Click here for more information about adding networks.

Twitter	Add Network	Friendster	Add Network
Facebook	Add Network	Koornk	Add Network
Facebook Pages	Add Network	Diigo	Add Network
MySpace	Add Network	YouAre	Add Network
Ning	Add Network	Multiply	Add Network
GTalk Status	Add Network	Yammer	Add Network
AIM Status	Add Network	Flickr	Add Network
Tumblr	Add Network	Utterli	Add Network
LinkedIn	Add Network	seesmic	Add Network
Identi.ca	Add Network	Laconi.ca	Add Network
Brightkite	Add Network	Present.ly	Add Network
FriendFeed	Add Network	Vox	Add Network
Plurk	Add Network	TypePad	Add Network
Jaiku	Add Network	ShoutEm	Add Network

9.9 When you first sign up with Ping.fm, you see the Manage Social Networks page with its incredible list of social networks supported by Ping.fm.

The idea is that you run through the list of social networks, and for each one you use, click the Add Network link and set up your account particulars. Here are the steps to follow for configuring Twitter on Ping.fm:

1. On the Manage Social Networks page, click the Add Network link beside Twitter.

The Settings / Twitter page appears, as shown in Figure 9.10.

> **P** > **Settings / Twitter**   Edit Profile | Settings | Recent Posts | My Media | Help
>
> Clicking the link below will tell Twitter that it's OK that we post messages to your page. If you don't have a Twitter account, you should probably get one before clicking the link.
>
> Click here to get your Twitter account. It's free!
>
> ### Link Ping.fm to Twitter

9.10 Use the Settings / Twitter page to connect Ping.fm to your Twitter account.

2. Click Link Ping.fm to Twitter. The Twitter authorization page appears.

3. If you aren't already signed in to Twitter, type your Twitter username and password.

4. Click Allow. Twitter links Ping.fm to your account and then returns you to the Manage Social Networks page.

5. Click Dashboard. The Your Dashboard page appears.

note   To add more networks, click Dashboard at the top of any Ping.fm page, and then click the Add More Networks link in the Social Networks section of the Dashboard page.

Getting your Ping.fm application key

If you plan on using Ping.fm with third-party applications such as twhirl (see the next section), iGoogle, or Facebook, then you need to provide those applications with your Ping.fm application key. Here's what you do:

1. Click Dashboard at the top of any Ping.fm page. The Your Dashboard page appears.

2. In the Services / Tools section, click Application Keys. The Application Keys page appears.

3. **Click the Desktop / Web Key value.** Ping.fm automatically selects the key.

4. **Press Ctrl+C (or ⌘+C on your Mac).**

5. **Open the third-party program, access the Ping.fm application, gadget, or whatever, and then paste the application key when prompted.**

Configuring twhirl to use Ping.fm

If you use the twhirl desktop client to post to Twitter, you can also use it to pass along your tweets to Ping.fm. Here's how:

1. **In twhirl, click Configuration (the wrench icon).** The Configuration dialog box opens.

2. **Display the General tab.**

3. **Select the Ping.fm check box.**

4. **Paste your Ping.fm app key.**

5. **Click Save.** twhirl saves your new settings and will now also send your tweets to your Ping.fm account.

Posting with Ping.fm

Posting a status update with Ping.fm is this easy:

1. **Click Dashboard at the top of any Ping.fm page.** The Your Dashboard page appears.

2. **Use the Ping My list to decide where you want the message to go:**

   - If you want to update all your networks that accept status updates (including Twitter), either leave the Default item chosen or choose Statuses.

   - If you only want to send the update to a single network (such as Twitter), choose that network in the list.

note The Ping.fm Default setting is usually Statuses, meaning that a ping gets sent to networks that accept status updates. To check this, click Settings, click Default Settings, and then choose Status Updates in the Default method list.

3. **Type your message in the large text box.**

4. **Click Ping it.**

You Are There: Geotagging Your Tweets

In Chapter 6, you learned how to search for tweets based on location. Similarly, a bit later in this chapter I tell you about a service called twittearth that offers a 3-D virtual globe that shows public timeline tweets by location.

You can search for tweets by location and twittearth can display tweets by location because many people fill in their Twitter account's Where In the World Are You? text box (click Settings, click the Account tab, and scroll down to the Location section). That's cool and all, but this system suffers from a few glaring problems:

- Some people don't fill in their location.
- Some people purposely fill in their location with an incorrect value (for example, a city they'd like to live in).
- Some people use fanciful or funny locations instead of real ones.
- Some people move around during the day, so although their location may be correct when they tweet from home or the office, it may not be correct after they've traveled to some other place.

In other words, although Twitter's location data is somewhat useful, you can't be sure that it's accurate or that it reflects where people are actually tweeting from. Why is that a problem? Because location data combined with the immediacy of Twitter can be extremely useful:

- What concerts or live shows are going on right now in my city?
- What are people who are actually at the Super Bowl tweeting about the game?
- Has anyone tweeted about any of the restaurants in my neighborhood?
- During a major event such as the 2009 Iranian protests or the 2008 terrorist attacks in Mumbai, India, how can I view tweets from people who are actually on the scene?

To support these and many other location-based scenarios, Twitter offers a service called *geotagging* that enables Twitter clients to augment (that is, *tag*) their tweets with their current locations, as well to view the location data for other users' tweets. As I write this, Twitter says that geotagging will eventually come to the Twitter.com site, but for now it's only available via third-party clients, particularly mobile apps (covered later in this chapter).

Geotagging obviously has tremendous potential, but you see in the next section that Twitter turns off geotagging by default in all accounts. What's up with that? A few things, actually:

- It's one thing to share with people what you're having for lunch, but it's quite another to allow people to know exactly where you're having that lunch. For many people, giving away one's location with each tweet is a simple but unforgivable invasion of privacy.

- Even if you're cool with the overall privacy thing, geotagging can still be problematic if you happen to tweet from somewhere you shouldn't be. For example, if you called in sick to work and you later tweet from a movie theater, the geotag in that tweet could give you away. Similarly, if you're shopping for a special present for your spouse and you tweet your friends for a bit of help, giving away your location could spoil the surprise.

- If you always tweet from the same location in, say, Paris, Texas, and then one day all your tweets are coming from Paris, France, it will be obvious to everyone that you're out of town on a vacation or business trip. That's cool info for your friends to know, but it's not so cool for burglars and other nefarious types who will no doubt be trolling Twitter looking for such location changes.

note Twitter also supports a location-based feature called Local Trends that shows you trending topics from a particular country or city. Your home page sidebar includes a Trending section, which is initially set to Worldwide. If you see a Local Trends box appear beside the Trending section, click Set your location. (If you don't see this box, click the Trending section's Change link.) Click the country or city you want to monitor, and then click Done.

Enabling geotagging in your Twitter profile

If you've thought long and hard about whether you want your tweets geotagged and you've decided to go for it, then you need to follow these steps to enable geotagging on your Twitter account:

1. **Log in to your Twitter account.**
2. **Click Settings.** Your account's Settings page appears.

3. **Click the Account tab.**

4. **In the Tweet Location section, select the Add a location to your tweets check box, as shown in Figure 9.11.**

5. **Click Save.** Twitter saves the new setting, and your tweets are now geotaggable.

Tweet Location

☑ Add a location to your tweets

Ever had something you wanted to share ("fireworks!", "party!", "ice cream truck!", or "quicksand...") that would be better with a location? By turning on this feature, you can include location information like neighborhood, town, or exact point when you tweet.

When you tweet with a location, Twitter stores that information. You can switch location on/off before each tweet and always have the option to delete your location history. Learn more

You may delete all location information from your past tweets. This may take up to 30 minutes.

9.11 Access your Twitter settings and select the Add a location to your tweets check box to start doing the geotagging thing.

Playing with some geotagging tools

To get the most out of geotagging, you have to combine a Twitter client with some kind of so-called *location-aware* device, the most common of which nowadays is a GPS-enabled mobile phone (such as an iPhone). You give the device permission to use your location information, and it can then tag your tweets with your current coordinates. (Location-savvy clients also show you the location data embedded in incoming tweets.) Twitter's geotagging feature is only a couple of months old as I write this, so there aren't tons of clients that support the new feature (and, as I said earlier, Twitter.com doesn't do the geotagging thing yet, although that's just a matter of time). However, location-based tweeting is expected to be the Next Big Thing in the Twitterverse, so I'm sure there will be all kinds of location-aware apps before long. For now, though, here are a few Twitter geotagging tools to check out:

● **Twittelator Pro.** This iPhone app is loaded with geotagging- and location-related features. Tap Settings, scroll down to the GPS and Location section, and then tap the Use GPS and Geotag Tweets settings to On, as shown in Figure 9.12. (When the iPhone asks if it's okay for the program to use your location, be sure to tap OK.) If an incoming tweet has been geotagged, Twittelator Pro displays a red pushpin above the tweet; tap the pin to see the tweet location.

- **Birdfeed**. This is an iPhone Twitter client that has geotagging baked in. For example, when you compose a tweet, you see the Add a location to this tweet bar above the text box, as shown in Figure 9.13. If you want to geotag the tweet, just tap that bar (and then tap OK when iPhone OS asks you to confirm). If you open a geotagged tweet, Birdfeed tells you the user's street, city, and country, which is nice. What's not so nice (even a bit dumb, in fact) is that Birdfeed doesn't indicate in the timeline which incoming tweets have been geotagged.

- **Foursquare**. This very popular iPhone app lists locations in your area, and each location comes with a View Tweets Nearby command that you can tap to see a list of tweets that originated close to the location.

9.12 In Twittelator Pro's Settings screen, enable the Use GPS and Geotag Tweets options.

9.13 When you compose a tweet in Birdfeed, tap the Add a location to the tweet bar to geotag the tweet.

- **TweetDeck**. You can't (yet) use TweetDeck to geotag tweets, but the desktop version of the program is geotag aware. If it comes across a tweet that has embedded location data, it displays a yellow View location map icon beside the tweet date. Click that icon to see a map of the location, as shown in Figure 9.14.

- **Seesmic Web**. The Seesmic Web app doesn't yet support geotagging your tweets, but it does recognize incoming geotagged tweets. Such tweets display a beacon icon beside the timestamp, and hovering your mouse over the beacon displays the location map, as shown in Figure 9.15. You can also click the beacon to open a Google map of the location in a new browser window.

9.14 In the desktop version of TweetDeck, tap the View location map icon to see a tweet's geotagged location.

9.15 In the Seesmic Web app, hover the mouse pointer over the beacon icon to pop up a map showing the tweet's geotagged location.

Deleting your location data

The location data that gets embedded in your tweets is stored on the Twitter servers so that third-party tools can use it. If you decide that geotagging just isn't for you, you can easily turn it off (click Settings, click the Account tab, and then deselect the Enable geotagging check box). However, all that location data stays with your previously geotagged tweets even after you turn off this feature. To scrub the location data from your old tweets, you need to follow these steps:

1. **Log in to your Twitter account.**

2. **Click Settings.** Your account's Settings page appears.

3. **Click the Account tab.**

4. **In the Tweet Location section, click Delete all location information.** Twitter asks you to confirm.

5. **Click OK.** Twitter proceeds to clean out your location data, which could take as long as a half-hour or so.

Connecting to Third-Party Twitter Applications

Most Twitter tools require access to your Twitter account so that they can retrieve your various timelines and enable you to access and update your profile data, follow and unfollow users, enable you to post tweets, and so on. In Twitter's early days, this meant that you had to fork over your Twitter username and password, a scary prospect at the best of times because of the potential for abuse. If you were sure the third party was legit, you could hand over your login credentials without a second thought, but with new Twitter tools springing up daily, who could tell which ones were aboveboard and which ones were up to no good?

Inevitably, lots of Twitter accounts were compromised by folks giving out their usernames and passwords to various nogoodniks, so finally Twitter decided to do something about it. It implemented a new method for connecting third-party tools to Twitter accounts. This new method uses the Open Authentication Protocol — almost always abbreviated to OAuth — where access to your account is controlled via a special connection with Twitter itself. Most importantly, with OAuth you never have to give out your username and password to third-party sites and tools. Instead, you just tell Twitter to give a third party access to your account, and you can easily revoke that access at any time.

caution OAuth is a much safer way to connect with third-party Twitter tools, but it's not a universal solution. You'll still have to give out your Twitter username and password to some tools that enable you to post tweets, particularly desktop and mobile apps. Be careful who you give out your credentials to, and if you notice any odd activity on your accounts — particularly tweets and direct messages you didn't send yourself and follow/unfollow actions that you didn't initiate — then you should immediately reset your Twitter password.

Connecting using OAuth

Twitter has been encouraging third-party developers to use OAuth for some time now, so it's fairly common to see account connections require OAuth verification instead of your username and password. You'll know this is the case when you see a link for connecting to your Twitter account instead of the standard username and password text boxes. For an example, check out the Link Ping.fm to Twitter link shown earlier in Figure 9.10.

When you click such a link, Twitter usually displays an OAuth page similar to the one shown in Figure 9.16. Type your Twitter credentials to log in (remember that in this case you're sending your login credential to Twitter, not the third-party tool), and then click Allow. (If you ended up on this page without intending it — that is, the third-party site sent you here without your knowledge — you should click Deny because clearly the tool is up to no good.)

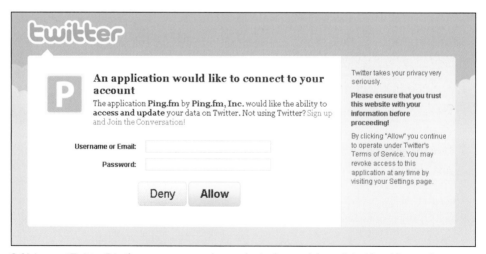

9.16 In most Twitter OAuth pages, you supply your login data and then click either Allow or Deny.

If you happen to be already logged in to your Twitter account, you see an OAuth page similar to the one shown in Figure 9.17. If you want to use a different account, click the Sign Out link and then log in with the correct credentials. When you're ready to proceed, click Allow.

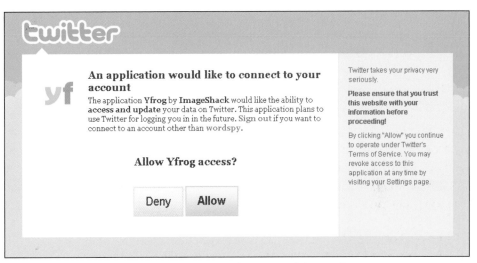

9.17 If you're already signed in to Twitter, you see this version of the OAuth page.

Revoking access

If you find that you no longer want to give a third-party site or app access to your Twitter account, you can revoke that access. Here's how it's done:

1. **Log in to your Twitter account.**
2. **Click Settings.** Your account's Settings page appears.
3. **Click the Connections tab.** Twitter displays all your OAuth connections, as shown in Figure 9.18.
4. **Click the application's Revoke Access link.** Twitter revokes the application's access to your account.

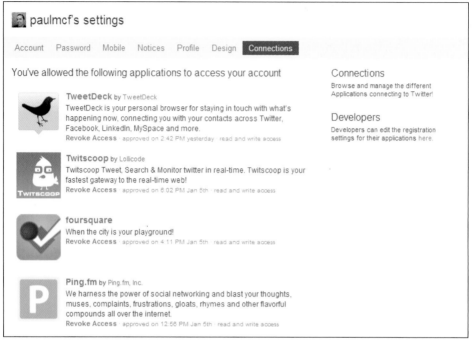

9.18 All your OAuth Twitter connections appear in the Connections tab.

More Twitter Tools to Play With

The Twitterverse is so crowded with Twitter-related tools that it would take another book this size, heck another *two* books this size, to cover them all. I might just do that one day, but for now I'll delve into a few tools that I think are useful, fun, or just plain cool.

Scheduling tweets

Sometimes you compose a tweet, but then realize it would be better if you posted it later. For example, it could be a birthday greeting or other message to a friend in a different time zone who, if you sent it now, might miss it because she's sleeping. Or perhaps you're going on vacation for a week and, not being a Twitterholic, you decide to also take a week off from tweeting. However, you don't want your account to appear dormant, so it would be nice to compose a few tweets now, and then have them posted every day or two while you're away.

Yes, Twitter is all about what's happening now, but sometimes your life is about what's happening then. For those times, you can take advantage of the growing list of services that let you schedule tweets. Here's a sampling:

- **FutureTweets (http://futuretweets.com).** With this service you can publish a tweet at a specific date and time, or you can set up a recurring tweet that gets shipped out daily, weekly, monthly, or yearly. Also includes the completely unrelated capability of flipping tweet text upside down and backward. No, I don't know why.

- **HootSuite (http://hootsuite.com).** This service lets you send tweets now or at a specified date and time. You can set up multiple Twitter accounts and perform most basic Twitter functions (send replies, retweets, and direct messages, unfollow people, see the replies and directs you've received, and more).

- **SocialOomph (www.socialoomph.com).** The free version of this service lets you post tweets a specific number of minutes, hours, days, or weeks from now, or at a specific date and time (see Figure 9.19). SocialOomph Professional (for which you must fork over a monthly fee) lets you create recurring tweets. Both versions also include many other tools for managing your Twitter life, including multiple Twitter accounts, automatic follows and unfollows, keyword tracking, and more.

caution

There's nothing wrong with scheduling tweets, but it's probably not something you want to overdo. There's an oddly impersonal quality to the whole exercise, so it feels sort of like getting your assistant to buy your spouse's birthday present.

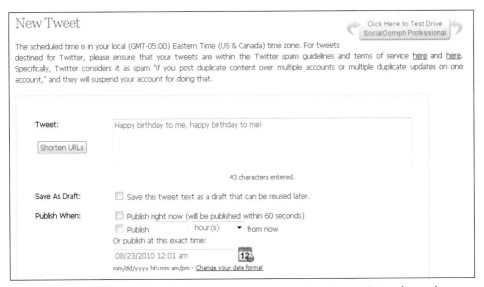

9.19 SocialOomph offers flexible scheduling options, so you can tweet now, minutes, hours, days, or weeks from now, or at a date and time that suit you.

Following Twitter trends

As a source of information, your everyday experience with Twitter probably consists of reading your friends' incoming tweets, and perhaps occasionally tuning in to the public timeline to marvel at the confusion and sheer incomprehensibility of it all. Looking at Twitter tweet-by-tweet it all seems so random, like so many atoms whooshing by.

However, just as atoms have a genius for combining into tangible objects, so too does the tweetstream produce its own order out of chaos. I'm talking here about Twitter trends, those topics and ideas that suddenly, without anyone planning anything or controlling anything, seem to be on everyone's Twitter lips.

Twitter itself mines the vast public database of tweets for interesting trends, and displays the top ten on the Twitter Search page (see Chapter 6). Of course, Twitter programmers want in on this action, too, so there's no shortage of tools that let you get a sense of the Twitter zeitgeist. Here are just a few to get you started:

- **Tweetmeme (http://tweetmeme.com).** This site examines the links in the tweetstream and shows which ones have been tweeted most often (see Figure 9.20).

- **Trendistic (http://trenddistic.com).** You can use this site to see how often a particular topic has been mentioned on Twitter, and you can even compare two or more topics.

9.20 Tweetmeme shows the most popular links on Twitter.

- **TwitScoop (www.twitscoop.com).** This addictive site offers a Buzzing right now feature that shows the most popular Twitter topics in a cloud format, where the more popular a topic is, the larger and bolder its text (see Figure 9.21). The addictiveness comes from the real-time display that shows topics growing and shrinking as you watch.

- **Twopular (http://twopular.com).** This site shows you the trending Twitter topics in different timeframes: the past two hours, eight hours, day, week, month, and ever since the service began (in late 2008). One nice touch is the use of up, down, and sideways arrows to indicate a trend's direction.

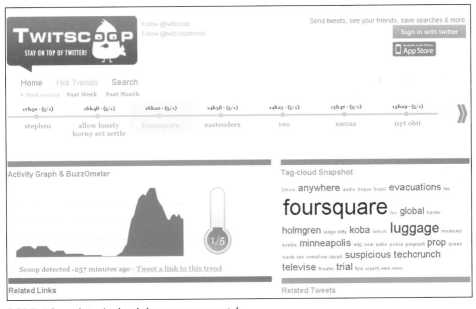

9.21 TwitScoop's topic cloud changes as you watch.

Tracking tweets by location

The next tool I'm going to tell you about comes with a warning: This site is so downright compelling that you should only visit on days when you have no pressing deadlines or other time constraints. That's because twittearth (http://twittearth.com/) grabs tweets randomly from the Twitterstream, and then displays the tweet text and its location on a gorgeous 3-D model of the earth, complete with cute little characters to represent the tweeters (see Figure 9.22). Two words: compulsively watchable.

A similar site is Twittervision (http://twittervision.com/), which offers both 2-D and 3-D maps of real-time tweets.

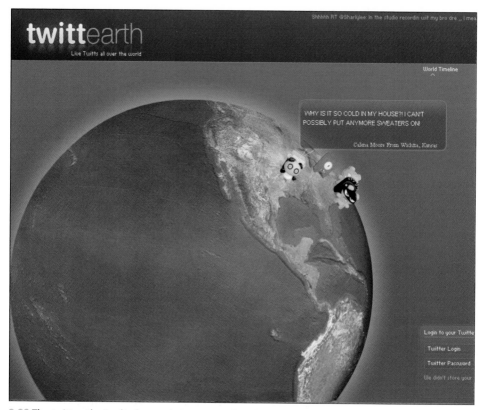

9.22 The twittearth site displays real-time tweets in 3-D.

Getting your Twitter account ranking

When a site turns up near the top of a Google search, that site is said to have lots of Googlejuice. So if your Twitter account is getting lots of buzz (followers, retweets, shout-outs, whatever), then I guess you could say that it's got lots of Twitterjuice. How would you know for sure, though? You could just go with what your gut tells you, but if you want something a bit less subjective, then I suggest you check out any of the following sites, which can tell you where you stand in the overall Twitter scheme of things:

- **TwInfluence (http://twinfluence.com/).** This site offers several interesting statistics that aim to measure your influence within the Twitterverse (see Figure 9.23). The top number is your overall influence rank and its percentile. Besides basic friends and followers numbers, you also get stats for your second-order followers (the total number of people your followers follow; also called *reach*); velocity (the rate at which your account is accumulating second-order followers); social capital (the average number of followers that your followers have); and centralization (a measure of how much of your total number of second-order followers is dependent on a few people with high followerships). There's lots of good math meat here if you have a taste for that kind of thing.

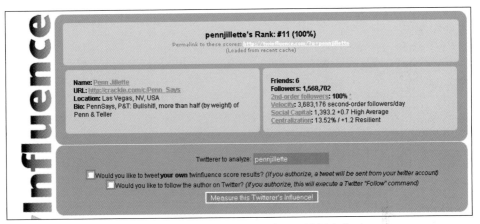

9.23 Find out how much influence you have in the twitosphere with TwInfluence.

- **Twitalyzer (http://twitalyzer.com/).** This site analyzes your overall influence in Twitter circles using four measures: signal-to-noise ratio (where *signal* refers to tweets that pass on information such as links and retweets, and *noise* refers to everything else); generosity (how often you retweet); velocity (the relative rate at which you post tweets); and clout (the relative rate at which other people reference your account in their tweets).

- **TwitterCounter (http://twittercounter.com).** This site shows your total number of followers and a graph of your followership growth over the past week. It also calculates the number of new followers you get per day and predicts how many you'll have in 30 days.

- **Twitter Grader (http://twitter.grader.com/).** This site delves deep into your Twitter data to provide you with an overall number that's supposed to show where you rank against all other Twitter users. The site offers no clue as to how this rank is calculated, so take the results with one or two grains of salt.

Displaying your latest tweet on a photo

SayTweet (http://saytweet.com/) qualifies as a tool if by the word *tool* you mean "a silly, pointless, but just plain fun mashup that you can display on your Web site." The idea is that you upload a photo (or provide a photo URL) to SayTweet, click that photo, and then provide your Twitter username. At the spot you clicked, SayTweet adds a speech bubble, and your most recent tweet appears in that bubble. The site then provides you with some code to add to your site, and visitors see your photo and speech-bubble tweet, as shown in Figure 9.24. Silly? Check. Pointless? Check. Just plain fun? Check.

9.24 Use SayTweet to display your latest tweet in a speech bubble on a photo. Why not?

Tweeting events to your Google calendar

Do you keep your life running smoothly by using Google Calendar (http://google.calendar.com/) to track your appointments, meetings, three-martini lunches, and other events? If so, you'll be happy to know that you can also keep your life running smoothly from the Twittersphere by taking advantage of a tool that lets you update Google Calendar via Twitter.

Twittercal (http://twittercal.com/) is a service that lets you update your Google Calendar using a direct message on Twitter. You follow @gcal on Twitter, provide Twittercal with your Twitter username and Gmail address, and then authorize Twittercal to access your Google Calendar.

When all that's done, you send a direct message to @gcal to add events to your calendar. You use Google Calendar's Quick Add syntax, which is described in glorious detail here:

http://www.google.com/support/calendar/bin/answer.py?answer=36604

Integrating your Twitter account with LinkedIn

If you have a LinkedIn account (www.linkedin.com), you probably find it a useful tool for making new business contacts. However, you can also use it to track tweets that mention your company and to link to your Twitter account.

Using LinkedIn to track tweets about your company

Sign on to LinkedIn, click More, and then click Application Directory. Click the Company Buzz application to open the preview page, and then click Add application. Company Buzz automatically adds topics that cover your LinkedIn profile data, such as your company name, the names of previous employers, and your school names. You can also add other topics to track them within LinkedIn.

Adding a link to your Twitter account on your LinkedIn profile

If you've got a LinkedIn network on the go and your tweets are work related (or are in some way related to your LinkedIn profile), then you can add your Twitter account to your LinkedIn profile. Here are the steps to follow to connect your Twitter account to your LinkedIn profile:

1. **Go to http://www.twitter.com/ and log in to your account.**

2. **Navigate to http://www.linkedin.com/ and log in to your account.**

3. **Click Settings.** The Settings page appears.

4. **Click Twitter Settings.** The Twitter Settings page appears.

5. **Click Add your Twitter account.** The Twitter authorization page appears.

6. **Click Allow.** Your Web browser sends you back to the Twitter Settings page on LinkedIn, and you see your Twitter account.

7. **If you want to show your tweets on your LinkedIn profile, select the Yes, visible to anyone option.**

8. **Select one of the following options to determine how your tweets are shared with your LinkedIn network:**

   - **Yes, visible to anyone.** Select this option to share all your tweets with your LinkedIn friends. This is the way to go if all or most of your tweets will be of interest to your network.

● **Share only tweets that contain #in.** Select this option to share with your LinkedIn network only those tweets that include the text "#in" somewhere in the tweet. This is the option to choose if you want to control which tweets get shared with your network.

9. **Click Save.**

Send your blog feed to Twitter

If you have a blog as well as a Twitter account, you can send a tweet each time you post a new blog entry to let your followers know you have some outside content for them to read. However, why bother with that extra step when you can get your blog post sent automatically to your Twitter account? The tool for this task is Twitterfeed (http://twitterfeed.com/), which takes items in from an RSS feed and automatically forwards them to a Twitter account.

Here's how you set things up:

1. **Go to http://twitterfeed.com/ and create an account.**

2. **Click Create new feed.** Twitterfeed displays the New Feed page.

3. **Use the Feed Name text box to type the name of the feed.**

4. **Type the address of your blog's feed in the RSS Feed URL text box.** To make sure all's well, I suggest clicking Test RSS feed to ensure that Twitterfeed is receiving the feed loud and clear.

5. **Click Advanced Settings.** Twitterfeed displays the advanced feed settings.

6. **Use the Update Frequency list to choose how often you want Twitterfeed to check your RSS feed for new entries.**

7. **Use the Include list to choose what parts of each blog post you want posted to Twitter.** Choose title & description, title only, or description only.

Because tweets are limited to 140 characters and most blog posts are much larger than that, the title only option is usually the way to go here.

8. **If you don't want your update to include a link back to your blog, deselect the Post Link check box.** If, instead, you decide to include the link, use the Shorten link through list to choose an URL-shortening service.

9. If you want to mark these tweets to indicate they come from your blog (for example, "Blog Post:"), type up to 20 characters in the Post Prefix text box. Figure 9.25 shows a feed just about ready for action.

10. Click Continue to Step 2.

11. In the Available Services list, click Twitter.

12. Click Authenticate Twitter and then click Allow when the OAuth page appears.

13. Click Create Service. Twitterfeed creates your new feed.

Twitterfeed checks your blog feed after whatever time interval you chose in Step 6, and it then posts your most recent blog entry to your Twitter account.

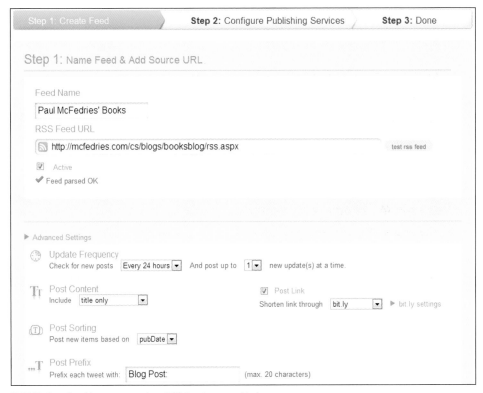

9.25 Twitterfeed lets you send an RSS feed to your Twitter account.

glossary

@username A reference to a Twitter user.

avatar The user icon associated with a Twitter account.

badge A small graphic with a Twitter-inspired design that you use as a link to your Twitter home page.

bot An automated Twitter account that returns some kind of data in response to a specially formatted message.

celebritweet A celebrity or famous person who uses Twitter.

curate To create and maintain a list of Twitter users.

direct To send a direct message to someone; a direct message.

direct message A private note that only the recipient can read.

egoTwittering Searching for your name on Twitter.

exactotweet See *twoosh*.

fail whale The page that Twitter displays when it is over capacity and can't accept any more tweets.

favorite To save a tweet for later viewing; a tweet saved to your favorites timeline.

follow To connect with a Twitter user to see that person's updates in your friend timeline.

followership The people who follow a particular Twitter user.

follow ratio The ratio of the number of people that a user follows with the number of people who follow the user.

followorthy Worthy of being followed on Twitter.

friend timeline The list of tweet posts by the people you follow.

geotagging Augmenting a tweet with your current location; viewing the location data for other users' tweets.

hashtag A word that, when preceded by a hash (#), defines or references a topic on Twitter.

hypertweeting Posting an excessive number of tweets.

live-tweeting Sending on-the-fly updates that describe or summarize some ongoing event.

location-aware Describes hardware or software that can work with location data, such as the coordinates generated by GPS (Global Positioning System) devices.

mashup Information created by combining data from two or more different sources.

meme A cultural artifact, such as an idea or catchphrase, that spreads quickly from person to person.

mention An update that includes a tweeter's @username.

microblogging Posting short thoughts and ideas to an online site such as Twitter.

mutual follow When two people on Twitter follow each other.

OAuth A security protocol that enables you to connect third-party sites and tools to your Twitter account without giving out your Twitter username and password.

oversharing Sending too many tweets in a short period of time; posting tweets that include overly personal or trivial details of one's life.

partial retweet A retweet that includes only part of the original tweet.

reply A response to a tweeter's update.

retweet Another person's tweet that you copy and send out to your followers, along with an acknowledgment of the original tweeter.

RT An abbreviation used to mark an update as a retweet; a retweet.

timeline A related collection of tweets, sorted by the date and time they were posted.

tweeple People who use Twitter.

tweeps A Twitter user's friends.

tweet An update posted to Twitter.

tweet cred Twitter credibility.

tweeter A person who uses Twitter.

tweetstream The tweets in a timeline.

tweetup A real-world meeting between two or more people who know each other through the online Twitter service.

tweetwalking Writing and posting a Twitter update while walking.

tweme A Twitter meme.

tweople See *tweeple*.

Twitosphere See *Twitterverse*.

Twittaholic A person who uses Twitter compulsively.

Twitterati The Twitter users with the most followers and influence.

Twitterer A Twitter user.

Twitterpated Overwhelmed by incoming tweets.

Twitterrhea The act of posting an excessive number of tweets in a short time.

Twittersphere See *Twitterverse*.

Twitterstream See *tweetstream*.

Twitterverse The Twitter social networking service and the people who use it.

Twitticism A witty tweet.

Twittiquette Twitter etiquette; an informal set of guidelines and suggestions for updating, following, replying, and sending direct messages.

twoosh A tweet that is exactly 140 characters long.

tword A new word created by appending "tw" to an existing word.

unfollow To stop following a Twitter user.

URL-shortening service A Web site or program that converts a Web address into a much shorter URL and then uses that URL to redirect users to the original address.

verified account An account where the tweeter's identity has been verified by Twitter.

Notes

Notes

index

The Genius is in.

978-0-470-29052-1

978-0-470-29050-7

978-0-470-42348-6

978-0-470-38760-3

978-0-470-29061-3

978-0-470-38108-3

978-0-470-29169-6

978-0-470-29170-2

The essentials for every forward-thinking Apple user are now available on the go. Designed for easy access to tools and shortcuts, the *Portable Genius* series has all the information you need to maximize your digital lifestyle. With a full-color interior and easy-to-navigate content, the *Portable Genius* series offers innovative tips and tricks as well as savvy advice that will save you time and increase your productivity.

Available wherever books are sold.

WILEY
Now you know.